# Teens and Gambling

## Who Wins?

Patricia Haddock

— Issues in Focus —

**ENSLOW PUBLISHERS INC.**

| | |
|---|---|
| 44 Fadem Road | P.O. Box 38 |
| Box 699 | Aldershot |
| Springfield, NJ 07081 | Hants GU12 6BP |
| U.S.A. | U.K. |

*The names of all gamblers in this
book have been changed.*

**Library of Congress Cataloging-in-Publication Data**

Haddock, Patricia.
    Teens and gambling : who wins? / Patricia Haddock.
       p. cm. — (Issues in focus)
    Includes bibliographical references and index.
    Summary: Explores the benefits and drawbacks of gambling, includes
personal accounts of teens who have had gambling problems, and discusses
the business of gambling and how technology has promoted it.
    ISBN 0-89490-719-0
    1. Gambling—United States—Juvenile literature. 2. Compulsive gambling—
United States—Juvenile literature. 3. Teenagers—United States—Juvenile
literature. [1. Gambling. 2. Obsessive-compulsive disorder.] I. Title. II. Series:
Issues in focus (Hillside, N.J.)
    HV6715.H33 1996
    363.4'2'0835—dc20                     95-39273
                                       CIP
                                       AC

Printed in the United States of America

10 9 8 7 6 5 4 3 2

**Illustration Credits:** The Las Vegas News Bureau, pp. 46, 66; Momo Photo
and Imaging, pp. 7, 15, 33, 40, 51, 53, 77, 82, 87, 91, 92; P.A. Haddock,
pp. 49, 55, 59, 63, 71; World Museum of Mining, Butte, MT, pp. 26, 27,
29.

**Cover Illustration:** The Stock Market, © 94 J. Barry O'Rourke.

# Contents

# Acknowledgments

Many thanks to my sister, Bev, who fed the cats, cooked the dinners, did the dishes, and provided encouragement; to Susan Rogers, for her editorial and research assistance; to Momo of Momo Photo and Imaging, for her excellent photographs and assistance with artwork; to Dave Johns for historical photos; to Ed Looney and the Council on Compulsive Gambling of New Jersey; to Susan Netboy of Greyhound Friends for Life; and to the Humane Society of the United States.

*Whoever plays deep must necessarily lose his money or his character.*

—Lord Chesterfield, *Letters to His Godson*, 1773

# 1

# You Win Some, You Lose Some

Being a teenager today is risky business. Teens have to watch out for gangs, drugs, alcohol, AIDS. And now they have to watch out for gambling, too.

As a teenager, John played cards for money. Innocent enough, except that John liked gambling and couldn't stop. When he ran out of his money to gamble with, he stole money from his mother.

John moved on to sports betting—betting on the outcomes of football, basketball, and hockey games. At sixteen, he began sneaking into the casinos in Atlantic City, and started playing for higher and higher "stakes"—something of value. Even though he was too young to play legally, the casinos treated him as a "high-roller"—someone who spends more than $5,000 a day on gambling. The casinos gave him free accommodations, alcohol, and other benefits. John kept coming back—and he kept losing. Eventually, John owed more than $100,000 in gambling debts, and he "graduated" to major crime to fund his gambling activities. When he was twenty-one years old, John was arrested for embezzlement and theft.[1]

Angela spent more than $5,000 of her and her family's money gambling. By the time she was seventeen, she was a preferred client at Atlantic City casinos. Even though her father informed the casinos that Angela was a minor and asked them to bar her from the casino floor, Angela continued to receive perks from the casinos. These perks included limo rides, free accommodations, meals, concert tickets, and drinks. By the time the casinos barred her from gambling, Angela had lost her entire college savings and was addicted to gambling.[2]

## Compulsive Gambling Starts Young

Each year, casinos identify and turn away more than two hundred thousand teen gamblers who try to enter. Another twenty thousand are ejected after they manage to get inside and are discovered.[3] But some teens like Angela and John, who make an effort to look more than twenty-one, beat the security system.

Have you ever bet money that you could shoot ten straight hoops, or win a foot race, or that the 49ers would win the Super Bowl? If so, you were gambling. You gamble when you play a game for stakes. You run the risk of losing your "wager" or bet. You run this risk in order to win the stakes. Using one of the above examples, if you win the foot race, you get the money. If you lose the foot race, you lose the money.

Pogs are another example of betting. Would you think that this game, using milk caps and slammers is gambling? It is. Today Pogs is big business—and a lot of it involves gambling.

Since Pogs became popular, as Michael Marr,

Pogs are big business. Originally, Pogs were milk caps from the Haleakala Dairy in Hawaii. Pogs stands for Passion Orange Guava.

author of "PogMania: A Tale of an Industry Gone Wild," reported, "Millions of dollars (in the form of dimes and quarters) [has] changed hands. Early on, most of it was 'kid money' exchanged for old-fashioned milk covers. As the phenomenon rocketed upward, $5 and $10 bills replaced loose change. . . ."[4]

For most people, betting among friends for loose change is usually pretty harmless. Casual gambling and wagering small sums are not usually bad behavior. Everyone gambles in one way or another. Games of chance fascinate most people. We experience a rush when we go against the odds and win. Carnival games at state fairs are a good example of fun gambling. You

# Games and Activities

You can bet on just about anything. Here's a partial list of games and activities that can involve gambling:

| | | |
|---|---|---|
| Backgammon | Computer games | Jai Alai |
| Baseball | Cribbage | Lotteries |
| Basketball | Dice | Pogs |
| Beauty pageants | Dog racing | Rodeos |
| Bingo | Football | Roulette |
| Bullfighting | Golf | Slot machines |
| Card games | Hockey | Soccer |
| Chess | Horse racing | Sports |

put down some money, try your skill at tossing a few rings, and—if you're dexterous enough—you win a stuffed pig or bunny. But compulsive gambling can cause behavior problems and lead to illegal activity.

## Three Types of Gamblers

Experts have identified three types of gamblers:

**Social and recreational gamblers.** These gamblers set aside a predetermined amount of time and money for gambling. They can stop gambling at any time, and usually save any winnings or use them to buy something special such as a CD player or to pay for a night on the town. Most people who gamble are this type.

**Problem gamblers.** These gamblers spend a great deal of time and money on gambling. They may wager more than they can afford, and may find it hard to stop gambling. Usually they gamble away their winnings. Problem gamblers may become compulsive gamblers.

**Compulsive gamblers.** Compulsive gambling is an addiction—an activity that a person has an uncontrollable urge to perform and finds extremely difficult to avoid performing. As with all addictions, compulsive gamblers develop a tolerance for their addictions—in this case, gambling. This means that compulsive gamblers need to make larger and more frequent bets to obtain the same kick. The gamblers feel greater and greater urges to gamble and are less and less able to resist temptation. Eventually, gambling affects the gamblers' ability to function in almost every aspect of their life.

People who come from families with alcohol, drug, or gambling problems are particularly vulnerable. So are those people who are in recovery from other types of addictions.

## Compulsive Gambling

Approximately twelve million people in America are considered compulsive gamblers; one million of them are teenagers.[5] The number grows daily. While the current ratio of male to female gamblers is 5 to 1, more women are joining the ranks of gamblers, since many women now have the time, money, and freedom to gamble. According to experts, women usually begin gambling as adults; men start gambling as children. Some people never stop betting and go on to become compulsive gamblers.

Many experts consider gambling as addictive and socially destructive as narcotics and alcohol addiction. Despite these facts, over the past ten years, citizens in state after state have voted for government-sponsored gambling activities.

In addition, the medical profession has recognized compulsive gambling as a disease, just like alcoholism or narcotics addiction are recognized diseases. According to medical professionals, compulsive gamblers have a psychological disease that is often unrecognized and, thus, goes untreated.

Typically, compulsive gamblers start their gambling

careers small. But $5 bets quickly become $500 bets; losses of $1,000 mushroom into losses of $100,000 or more. Compulsive gamblers start by gambling for a few hours, and end up spending days at the betting tables or race track. No matter what happens, no matter how big the loss, they convince themselves that the next big win is right around the corner.

Most demonstrate the following characteristics:

**Self-importance.** Gamblers tend to brag and exaggerate their self-importance. This often hides a basic insecurity and sense of inferiority. Casinos cater to this need by offering perks such as free rooms or meals.

**Sensitivity.** Gamblers are extremely sensitive to criticism and may react with rage or total dismissal when confronted about their gambling.

**Entitlement.** Gamblers believe they are entitled to special treatment from everyone else and feel disappointed when they aren't treated with deference.

**Fantasy.** Gamblers daydream about making it big, but they often don't back up their dreams with hard work. If they do succeed, they will often dismiss the achievement.

**Envy.** Gamblers often envy others who seem to have more luck or success than they do.

**Recognition.** Gamblers need attention and recognition. They often do favors or give gifts in order to obtain the approval of others.

**Uniqueness.** Gamblers often think no one else has the problems they do, so, they usually don't seek help.

Often, gamblers are taught as children that having

money equals self-esteem and power. They tend to be unable to defer gratification and want what they want right now, regardless of the consequences.

Lillian started gambling as a teen when she flipped baseball cards and shot dice. As Lillian grew older, she added poker, pool, backgammon, and sports bets to her gambling repertoire. Once, instead of picking up her eleven-year-old son, she left him standing on a street corner for three hours while she played cards.

Compulsive gamblers are often bright successful people who go to great lengths to disguise their addiction. But it always catches up to them. They exhaust their resources and hit rock bottom with no rescue in sight.

The freefall of gambling has been described by Deke Castleman in his book *Las Vegas*. He says:

> A gambling disorder starts out as a euphoria derived from the excitement of the activity—a more satisfying sensation than anything else these people have experienced. . . . As long as these people gamble, they're riding high; stopping means coming down, and they need to gamble to get back up. . . . Nearly all compulsive gamblers spend their own and their families savings. Three out of four sell or hock valuables, and write bad checks. Almost half descend to theft or embezzlement. . . . An estimated 20% of compulsive gamblers attempt suicide.[6]

At least half of all compulsive gamblers resort to illegal activities to fund their gambling. They write bad checks, file phony insurance claims, or embezzle money. Research at two prisons in New Jersey shows that more than 30 percent of prisoners were pathological gamblers and half of them were in jail for gambling-related crimes.

David started gambling in elementary school. He stole change from his mother's purse to bet on baseball games. As a teen, he bet on card games; and in college, he discovered bookmakers and horse racing. As a businessman, he visited his first casino. David was hooked. He vacationed only in places where he could gamble. Eventually, he began breaking the law and consorting with gangsters to fund his gambling activities.

One day in 1975, David arrived in Las Vegas with $17,000 that he had won at the race track. He started playing 21 and hit a streak of luck, running the $17,000 up to $111,000! He needed the money, since he was under indictment for a stock market swindle and had heavy legal fees to pay. But David never made it home with his six-figure win. He lost the entire $111,000 in four additional hours of gambling. Plus, he lost another $25,000. "I knew I was doing bad things," he recalls. "I was a liar and a thief. But the monkey was on my back, and I needed a fix."[7]

Mike started gambling when he was ten. His uncle, a bookie, took Mike to the track and let the boy pick a horse. The uncle placed a $2 bet for him. The horse won $12, and Mike was hooked. He continued gambling throughout his teens and into college. As an adult, Mike would come home every night and rush to call his bookie to place a bet for that evening. He bet heavily on sports events for fourteen years, running up gambling debts of $250,000. He mortgaged his home, borrowed from relatives, pawned his and his wife's wedding rings, torched two cars to collect the insurance money, and embezzled $80,000 from his employer.

According to Valerie Lorenz, Ph.D., executive director for the National Center for Pathological Gambling in Baltimore, MD, "Without help, the illness becomes chronic and progressive, eventually leading to financial ruin, broken homes, and a very high suicide rate."[8]

## Costs of Compulsive Gambling

The costs of compulsive gambling are high:

- Disruption of family, including divorce
- Abused or neglected children
- Impoverishment
- Mental breakdown
- Lost productivity through absenteeism, wasted time, poor performance
- Criminal activities
- Fear, depression, attempted suicide

Winning just fuels the addiction because the compulsive gambler never wins enough. They have to keep trying for the big one. Win or lose, the compulsive gambler is never satisfied, never happy. "Emotionally, the gambler turns ornery—tense, irritable, argumentative, or conversely withdrawn—particularly while looking for the next game," reports a *Newsweek* article. "Professionally, work becomes the activity that fills time between bets. And financially, trouble builds, as spending turns into borrowing and borrowing spirals

Horse racing is a major type of gambling.

out of control into stealing."[9] For example, David was rarely home with his wife or children. And when he was home, he was often furious and in a tirade over his gambling losses.

Gamblers don't gamble for money alone. If they did people such as Lillian, David, and Mike would quit when they win. But they don't quit. They keep gambling for the rush that comes from the risk, from living on the edge. Science has discovered that gambling produces a response in the brain that is similar to that produced by heroin, sex, and chocolate. Says one gambler in an interview in *The New York Times Magazine*, "Gambling for someone like me has nothing to do with winning or losing. . . . The point is to be in the action—to risk everything, to have a bet that can wipe you out. That's when I get a real rush."[10]

Experts on compulsive gambling believe that the United States is building a nation of gamblers. Many states not only have legalized gambling activities such as lotteries and casinos but actively promote participation in these activities. Lotteries and casinos publicize the winners and the amounts won, but not the losses and bad odds. This type of publicity influences gamblers and encourages them to think that they have a shot at winning. Their lottery ticket or slot machine could be the next one to hit it big.

Jeremy started playing the lottery for fun; it seemed harmless. Lottery ads publicized big winners, and he believed the advertising slogans. He became addicted, losing $75,000 over a ten-year period, during which he told lies and stole money to fund his habit.

Advertising plays a role in encouraging gambling by getting players to believe the fantasy of the advertising. Advertising touts the big winners, not the awful odds. This type of skewed advertising is especially harmful to young people, who tend to believe in advertising more than adults. If a private business used the advertising tactics state lotteries do, government regulatory agencies such as the Federal Trade Commission (FTC) would step in. Unfortunately, lotteries are exempt from FTC regulation by order of Congress. They can pretty much do what they want.

Most teenage gamblers are boys who try their hand at gambling, then move on to other, less dangerous activities. Some teens, however, like to gamble. They like the rush that comes with risk. According to seventeen-year-old Larry, "You don't do it [gambling] for the money. . . . You do it for the action."[11] In addition, availability of slots and "rub-off" instant lotteries contribute to turning casual gamblers into compulsive ones.

For some people—such as the adults and teens discussed in this chapter—gambling is addictive. Once they start wagering, they can't stop. Lives and families have been ruined because of gambling, and the number of teen gamblers is increasing alarmingly.

## Compulsive Teen Gamblers

Durand Jacobs, a psychologist and vice president of the National Council on Problem Gambling,

17

conducted a survey of twenty-seven hundred high school students. Half of the students reported gambling at least once a year. Thirteen percent financed their gambling activities by committing crimes such as stealing. Five percent were considered pathological gamblers who had been arrested for gambling-related activities. Translated into national figures, more than one million teens are problem or compulsive gamblers.[12]

Here are some characteristics of problem and compulsive teen gamblers. They:

- Withdraw from family and friends, especially those from whom they have borrowed or stolen money.
- Lose interest in schoolwork and hobbies, preferring to follow sporting events on which they have placed wagers.
- Have money that doesn't come from wages or allowances.
- Resort to theft or burglary, or sell drugs to finance gambling activities.
- Lie and cheat to cover their tracks.
- Become impulsive and rebellious.
- Neglect family, job, and school responsibilities.
- Have problems with the law.
- Abandon old friends to spend time with gambling teens.
- Cut school to gamble.
- Stop studying.
- Are restless and irritable when not gambling.
- Use the telephone at specific times of the day to place bets.
- Get into trouble with professional criminals when they place bets with bookmakers.

- Sell prized possessions such as CDs, sporting equipment, or musical instruments to cover bets.

- Spend free time gambling.

- Brag abut gambling winnings.

- Use gambling jargon such as "bookie," "loan shark," "point spread," "bet."

- Have an unexplained need for money.

- Hold regular card games with friends.

- Experience severe mood swings.

Why do teens gamble? Partly because it's easy. Some form of gambling is legal in forty-eight states, and legal age limits vary from eighteen to twenty-one—depending on the state. Many lottery vendors don't ask for identification, so teens who look older can gamble illegally. In some states teens can buy lottery tickets at machines where there is no adult supervision. Teen gamblers often suffer from low self-esteem and may be obsessed with the need for having money. For compulsive gamblers, gambling seems to offer an easy solution to insufficient money, low self-esteem, boredom, and feelings of failure and defeat.

Problem and compulsive teen gamblers feed on the danger of being underage and trying to pass as older than they are. They get hooked on the high, sometimes faster than adults. In a survey of teens, results showed that 32 percent gamble every week, 8.8 percent are problem gamblers, and 3.8 percent are pathological gamblers. "More teens than ever before are addicted to gambling," states Ed Looney, executive director of the Council on Compulsive Gambling of New Jersey.

"Gambling activities are more available and gambling is promoted more today."[13]

Carl placed $200 bets each week with a book-maker. When his debt hit $8,000, the bookie threatened to amputate his mother's legs if he didn't pay off his debts. Carl's mother paid up for him. Dwight owed his bookie so much money, his parents had to sell their home to pay his debts.

## Do You Have a Gambling Problem?

To find out if you have a gambling problem, ask yourself these questions from the Council on Compulsive Gambling of New Jersey:

- Do you lose time from school due to gambling?
- Have your grades dropped because of gambling?
- Do you display intense interest in sports-related literature or sporting events on TV?
- Has gambling language or references increased in your conversation?
- Do you flash large amounts of money or show an exaggerated display of clothes or jewelry?
- Do you ever feel as if you were out of your own body when you gamble?
- Did you ever gamble to escape worry or trouble?
- Have your family or friends noticed a change in your behavior or personality (e.g., irritable, impatient, or sarcastic)?
- Do arguments, disappointments, or frustrations create within you an urge to gamble?
- Did you ever do anything illegal to finance your gambling?

If you think that you need help with a gambling

problem, look in your phonebook for the number of the local chapter of Gamblers Anonymous.

## Gambling Is Big Business

Legal gambling is big business.[14] Every state except for Utah and Hawaii allows some kind of legal gambling, and large corporations such as Hilton and MGM own gambling casinos.

How big is the gambling industry? Here are some startling statistics:

- Half a million people owe their jobs to the gambling industry.
- Ninety-five percent of all Americans live within driving distance of a casino.
- Americans wager more than $330 billion a year on legal gambling activities.
- Lottery sales total more than $24 billion a year.

Since states tax gambling money, legal gambling contributes billions of dollars to state treasuries. For example, most states keep eighty cents of every dollar wagered on lottery tickets.

Since the 1980s revenue-poor communities have looked to gambling as sources of revenue. This has served to legitimize gambling in the eyes of many Americans. So people who once would never consider wagering their money, willingly plunk down a dollar or five dollars for a lottery ticket. (There will be more about lotteries and casinos in Chapter 3.)

Each state regulates gambling activities, and most states have strict requirements about what is considered legal gambling and what isn't. What is considered legal in one state may not be legal in another. For example, for many years, casino gambling was legal in Nevada, but illegal in California. Now casinos on Indian reservations are legal in California and dozens of other states. (This subject will be more fully discussed in Chapter 4.)

Gambling creates jobs and revenue; it also creates problems. Some economists believe that gambling is a blight on local economies. Law enforcement agencies worry that legalized gambling leads to illegal activities.

Cheating and corruption are common problems that plague the gambling industry. The Federal Bureau of Investigation (FBI) estimates that more than $40 billion is wagered illegally in the United States. While big casinos are legitimate, *Newsweek* reported that criminals ". . . often run the businesses attracted by gambling, such as prostitution, loan-sharking and drugs. . . . Neighborhood bookies will always be more convenient than OTB [off-track betting] shops, and they don't report winnings to the IRS [Internal Revenue Service]. Gambling remains a training ground for mobsters."[15] (There will be more in Chapter 5 about problems with gambling.)

Is gambling good or bad for us as individuals and as a nation? There are arguments for both sides. You'll learn about some of them in the chapters that follow.

*The best throw of the dice is to throw them away.*

—English Proverb

# 2

# Gambling and Gamblers

Gambling is risky business. Its very nature caters to our desire to have a variety of experiences, some of which carry risk. In some cultures, gambling is an acceptable social activity. Many churches and clubs sponsor carnivals, games of chance, bingo games, and casino nights to raise money. Pauline Yoshishashi commented in *The Wall Street Journal,* "Gambling is a way of trying to beat the system, to get a risk-taking high while playing with important symbols of everyday life, like money."[1]

This characteristic of taking risks and bucking the odds is what makes some people disapprove of gambling. "It goes against the socially accepted norm of realistic and attainable goals achieved through conformity and hard work," David Spanier has commented in his book *Easy Money.*[2]

## More Popular Than Baseball

According to experts, gambling is more popular than baseball.[3] A poll of the general public—sponsored by Harrah's, a company that owns casinos—showed that 55 percent of Americans believe that "casino entertainment is perfectly acceptable for anyone." Thirty-five percent believe it's "acceptable for others, but not me." Only 10 percent consider gambling "not acceptable for anyone."[4]

Gambling has been around as long as people have.

- It was part of ancient religious rituals; supplicants threw objects such as bones or sticks and "read" the will of the gods by the manner in which the objects fell.

- Dice have been found in Egyptian tombs dating from 3,500 B.C., and were used in both ancient Greece and Rome.

- Loaded dice (weighted to fall unfairly) and games of chance were found in the ruins of Pompeii.

- Gambling is mentioned in the Bible. Moses cast lots to divide up the Promised Land among the twelve tribes. And Jonah was chosen by lot to be thrown overboard where he was swallowed by the whale.

- Romans bet on gladiators fighting in the Colosseum.

- Horse racing became known as the "Sport of Kings" because it was popular with royalty, and so expensive that only the rich could afford it.

- Dog racing, which dates from Roman times, is known as the "Sport of Queens" because it was a favored pastime at the court of England's Queen Elizabeth I.

## Taxation and Corruption

When Columbus's ships landed on the shores of what was to become America, the sailors brought cards and dice with them. Gambling played an important role in the formation of the thirteen colonies. While some colonists, such as the Puritans in Massachusetts and Quakers in Pennsylvania, passed laws against gambling, other colonies were more tolerant of private games. All the colonies, however, relied on lotteries as a legitimate financial tool for fund-raising.

Taxation was a sensitive issue to colonials. So using a lottery to raise money, where people voluntarily bought tickets, was much more acceptable. In colonial times a lottery resembled what we now call a raffle. People bought tickets rather than choosing numbers. A prize was awarded to the holder of the winning ticket. Benjamin Franklin organized a lottery to pay for military equipment, and the Continental Congress approved a lottery to help finance the American revolution.

Due to corruption, lotteries were banned starting in the 1830s. Money would be collected for public works, such as a building a new canal or bridge. But prizes were not always delivered, and the money was often stolen. The private companies that ran the lotteries made huge profits compared to what they paid to the state that was sponsoring the lottery.

As the country grew and new settlements sprang up, professional gamblers appeared. With the Louisiana Purchase, New Orleans joined the country. Soon French card games such as *faro* and *poque,* the forerunner

25

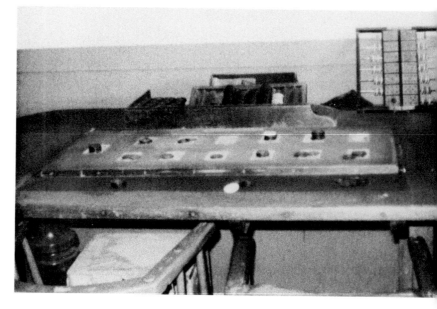

A nineteenth-century faro table.

of poker, became popular. The Mississippi River was a major commercial trade route for lumber, farm goods, and furs. Vessels of every kind floated down the river to New Orleans to have their cargo discharged. These vessels also carried gamblers with them.

The building of the railroads marked the end of the steamboat era. As the country expanded, gamblers moved to new frontiers. When gold was discovered in California, gamblers as well as miners flocked to San Francisco. Licensed gambling establishments opened and paid a percentage of their earnings to the city.

In mining towns across America, the gambling saloon provided a comfortable well-lit place to meet friends and socialize. Professional gamblers plied their

A nineteenth-century roulette table.

trade on unsuspecting travelers and prospectors. The towns grew, and many became "respectable." Soon law-abiding citizens campaigned against gambling and crime. Citizens banded together to confront the gamblers, and in town after town, passed anti-gambling laws. Gamblers fled to more lucrative areas.

At the turn of the century, gambling was illegal in most states. This didn't stop casino owners who paid off local politicians and police. Occasionally a gambling house would be raided by authorities. Usually the raid was prearranged and staged for the benefit of the public. Sometimes reform fever would sweep through an area. Or if someone was running for office and wanted votes, a real raid would close down a casino for a time.

## New Gambling Technology

Three technological advances helped promote and spread gambling. The first was the use of the telegraph for betting purposes. A bookie named Mont Tennes used a wire service to provide racing information to other bookies, who in turn paid him a percentage of their take. Bookmakers could do more business this way since they had access to more information more quickly.

The second invention to affect gambling was the pari-mutuel betting machine, invented in Paris. Before pari-mutuel betting, gamblers used independent bookies to place bets at race tracks. Since bookies controlled the betting, they also controlled the races, bribing jockeys and trainers, and cheating other bookies. With pari-mutuel betting, bettors wagered against each other rather than against a bookie, and could see the odds change as betting continued. Pari-mutuel betting is still popular today.

The third invention was the slot machine, invented in San Francisco in 1895. Slot machines soon appeared all over the country in drugstores, taverns, and gas stations. Various reform movements later made slot machines illegal outside of casinos, but you can still find illegal slots in many places.

Nevada eventually became the center for gambling

A nineteenth-century slot machine.

in the United States, starting in the 1930s. Today gambling is a nationwide activity, with some form of gambling legal in forty-eight states. (See Chapter 3 for information about lotteries and casinos, and Chapter 4 for the spread of casinos across America.)

Gambling is now mass-market entertainment. Its popularity is due to state and religious sanction; the proliferation of gambling throughout the United States through church bingo, lotteries, and legal casinos; advertisements that extol gambling as a way to get rich quick; and technology that can bring gambling right into our homes via a gambling cable network that will soon be launched.[5]

The opportunity to gamble is everywhere—from lottery machines in supermarkets to simulcasts of sporting events at race tracks. You can't get away from it. According to an article in *The Wall Street Journal:*

> Airlines are developing high-tech wagering while aloft through such devices as Virgin Atlantic's seatback video games. Cable and interactive television companies are planning ways to separate people from their money via television and phone lines. In some cities, racing fans already can wager by phone on their favorite nags, while lotteries and other gambling outlets are trying to figure out the logistics of at-home betting.[6]

Legal gambling is growing at about 10 percent a year; illegal gambling is also thriving. As accessibility and state-supported lotteries increase, so do the numbers of people who are starting to gamble. These newcomers start with a lottery ticket, then some move on to other types of gambling.

According to investment and industry forecasts, spending on gambling will double within a decade.[7] Riverboat gambling, card clubs, off-track betting parlors, and casinos are popping up all over, and will continue to do so. (See Chapter 4 for the spread of casinos across America.)

## The Gamblers

Many famous Americans were avid gamblers. Presidents George Washington, Thomas Jefferson, Andrew Jackson, and Martin Van Buren all liked to wager. Washington and Jefferson even kept journals of their winnings and losses.

Washington was reported to be a mediocre card player who limited his betting; Jefferson, on the other hand, died heavily in debt, mostly due to his spending on hospitality, but also, in part, to gambling. When he died, Jefferson was planning on raffling off his home, Monticello, to pay his debts.

With the advent of riverboats in the 1800s came the "gentleman gambler." By 1835, two hundred and fifty steamboats plied the Mississippi River and played host for two thousand gentleman gamblers. The riverboat gambler could be identified by his "uniform"—a dark broadcloth coat reaching to his knees, dark tightly fitted trousers, black hat, gaudy vest, and a ruffled shirt with a colorful tie. Diamond rings finished the outfit.

The riverboat gambler has been romanticized in American folklore, but in reality, many were cheats.

# A "Noble" Cardsharp

James "Jim" Bowie, one of the legendary heroes of the Alamo, was an adept gambler and enjoyed beating professional cheats at their own game. Once he boarded the steamboat New Orleans, where he witnessed a group of cardsharps working on a young planter. His inquiries revealed that the planter was returning home with his bride and $50,000 owed to friends and relatives. Bowie watched the young man lose all his money to the gamblers, then set to work getting it back.

Bowie made it known that he had a bankroll to spend, and the professional gamblers immediately got a poker game underway with Bowie in the "sucker" seat. After several hands, Bowie was dealt winning cards. The other gamblers bet up the pot, then dropped out one by one. Finally, only Bowie and one gambler remained. When the professional cardsharp reached up his sleeve where he had hidden a winning card, Bowie caught his hand and flashed his famous Bowie knife. The cheat folded his cards. Bowie won the pot of $70,000, returned $50,000 to the young man, and kept $20,000 for his efforts.

They counted on bored or naive travelers for their income. Poker was the most popular game on the riverboats, and gamblers were adept at "stacking" decks of cards. Using a deck of cards specially marked, the gambler could recognize key cards from the back. The riverboat gambler often worked with a partner to lure new prospects to the table. One would play the part of an unsophisticated player to make the prospect feel secure. They would let the prospect win a few times, encourage him to bet heavily, then use marked cards

A flush—five cards of the same suit—wins the poker hand.

to win the pot away from the unlucky prospect. Since many gamblers made their living by cheating, they had to be prepared to fight or flee when their hustling was discovered.

Despite the reality of their activities, gamblers such as James "Wild Bill" Hickok and Doc Holliday became legends in the last remaining outposts of the Wild West. Hickok, a U.S. marshal, was murdered in Deadwood, South Dakota, during a poker game. Doc

## The Stock Market Gamble

Not all gambling takes place in casinos or race tracks.[8] The stock and commodity markets offer the same kinds of fast-pace, financial risks, and thrills, and can be just as addictive as other, more traditional, forms of gambling.

According to Gordon Williams, writing in *FW*, "Plenty of Wall Street professionals, both brokers and traders, are in the business because they revel in the adrenaline rush that comes from gambling."[9] The successful Wall Street professional can have wealth, power, and the constant action that feeds the compulsive gambler. While this doesn't mean that all Wall Street stock and commodity traders are compulsive gamblers, many compulsive gamblers prefer to gamble on the stock and commodity markets rather than choosing another form of gambling such as casino gambling.

Holliday could handle a gun as smoothly as he handled cards. He was a feared dealer and gunfighter in the silver mining city of Tombstone, Arizona. Calamity Jane was also a card dealer and expert poker player.

## Why People Gamble

People gamble for many reasons. They do it for the fun and excitement, and to win money. Generally there are three types of gamblers: social, problem, and compulsive. Social gamblers can control their impulses to gamble. Problem and compulsive gamblers can't control the urge to gamble. Sociologists and authors Linda Berman and Mary-Ellen Seigel, who have studied gambling and gamblers, write: "Like alcohol or drugs, gambling can temporarily change a person's mood. . . . It [can] alleviate anxiety and depression . . . raise some people's self-esteem and given them a sense of identity. Those who begin as social or recreational gamblers are at risk of becoming problem or compulsive gamblers if they experience the gambling as a mood-changing 'drug' *and* have an extraordinary need to change their mood."[10] (There will be more discussion of problem and compulsive gamblers in Chapter 5.)

Gamblers come from all income brackets and occupations. Some are extremely competitive and independent risk takers; some are shy and reserved. Some are satisfied playing a penny slot machine; others are only happy if they are betting $1,000 on each turn of the cards. Here are some 1993 statistics about gamblers who have called the Council on Compulsive Gambling of New Jersey for help:

- Average gambling debt: $29,000
- Average annual income: $35,255
- Male gamblers: 75%
- Female gamblers: 25%
- Games played:
  - Casino games: 65%
  - Lotteries: 54%
  - Sports betting: 49%
  - Horse racing: 35%
  - Stocks and commodities: 5%
  - Bingo: 2%

*Adventure upon all the tickets in the lottery, and you lose for certain; and the greater the number of your tickets the nearer you approach to this certainty.*

–Adam Smith, The Wealth of Nations, 1776

# 3

# The Business of Gambling

These days, states are hard-pressed for money and politicians are reluctant to vote tax increases for fear of losing voters. The solution for many states is gambling. States raise money by sponsoring lotteries and taxing legal gambling activities, the most lucrative of which is casino gambling. This chapter looks at lotteries and casinos to see how and why they earn so much money for states and for the people who run them—but rarely for the gamblers who play the games.

## Lotteries

Lotteries helped to build our country.[1] They helped to finance the founding of Jamestown as well as Dartmouth and Princeton universities, and were popular ways of raising revenue until the turn of the century.

During the first half the twentieth century, Congress outlawed national lotteries. State legislators refused to consider them as legitimate sources of revenue for fear of voter backlash.

In the 1960s, however, New Hampshire opened the door to national gambling when voters approved a legal state lottery. Pro-lottery legislation spread slowly across the nation until the cash-poor decade of the 1980s when states lost government funding during Ronald Reagan's presidency. As federal government aid to states and cities dried up, state lawmakers found themselves with expensive programs to run—such as welfare, housing, education, and health care—and with no money to run them.

Few politicians had the courage to fund these programs by raising taxes, and no one wanted to cut benefits that voters felt that they were entitled to receive. Instead legislators looked for solutions that voters would find more acceptable. That solution was lotteries. In state after state, voters approved initiatives to create lotteries. Lotteries soon became the fastest growing source of state revenues in the 1980s.

## Winners and Losers

There are many different kinds of lottery games. The most common lottery is a Lotto-type game where players choose which numbers they think will come up in a random drawing.

Lotteries are popular with players because they offer the chance to win million-dollar payoffs. The first big lottery winner, Lou Eisenberg of Brooklyn, won $5 million in 1981. That's peanuts nowadays. The popularity of lotteries has spread across the nation and created an entirely new social class of million-aires—currently more than three thousand in all, with more being added each month. As some lotteries soar past nine digits, a few winners approach being called superrich.

For example, in 1993, a school teacher won $111 million in a multi-state lottery! A carpenter in Denver won $2 million *twice*! The odds of doing so are 17 trillion to 1! In 1991, the pot for the New York State lottery was $90 million. Retailers sold 61 million tickets in ten days—more than twenty-one thousand a minute near the end.

Multi-million dollar winnings are paid out over a twenty-year period, and winners obviously benefit from the money. Research shows that lottery winners have fewer divorces than nonwinners, usually don't become compulsive gamblers, and generally quit their jobs only to go back to school. So what's wrong with lotteries? Critics say plenty. Despite much publicity about big winners, most lottery players spend their lifetimes losing money by betting on the lottery.

Lottery revenues run about 40 percent, which means that of every dollar wagered, forty cents goes to the state; the other 60 percent goes to expenses and payouts. Many states justify a lottery to voters by allocating part

Tickets for the California lottery.

of their revenues to a worthy goal, such as education, housing, or historic preservation. Legislators recognized that voters who resisted tax hikes would eagerly approve a lottery, particularly if a portion of the proceeds went to a worthy cause. However, the lottery bonanza doesn't always produce the promised benefits.

After a lottery is up and running, the amount of money legislators would have set aside for the worthy cause often gets pared back or completely eliminated from the state's budget. In other words, lottery money doesn't always *add* to a state's allocation for that cause. Instead the state cuts back on what it already gives to that cause, so the net effect is a *wash*.

"In California, for instance, the lottery was established on the promise that 34 cents of every dollar would go to education," reports an article in *Fortune*. "'Schools Win Too' was the campaign slogan of pro-lottery forces in 1984. But since then . . . the money has simply replaced school funding rather than augmented it."[2] The result has been that voters refuse to pass education bond issues to raise funds because they think education has received a windfall from lottery proceeds. In Florida the percentage of total funding for education *decreased* since the state adopted a lottery. The very services that lotteries are supposed to benefit often turn out to be losers.

The poor also lose. Those who can least afford to gamble spend the most on lottery tickets. Research shows that in California, the poor spend fifteen times more of their income, as a percentage, on lottery tickets than the rich do.[3] Twenty percent of lottery players are responsible for 65 percent of the wagers.

In one California survey a mere 10 percent of the population bought more than half the tickets. A Maryland study showed that, among players earning under $10,000, the top 20 percent of this income bracket spent an average of more than $32 a week on lottery tickets.[4]

What about the promise not to raise taxes because of lottery income? In the past decade, taxes have been increased in every lottery state.

Lotteries also send the wrong message to young people. Instead of teaching young people the value of hard work and personal achievement, lotteries hold out a Cinderella promise. They cater to those who want to get rich the quick and easy way. For example, a commercial for the New York lottery showed a woman suggesting to her daughter that the daughter didn't have to study hard because the mom was going to win the lottery. George Will commented in *Newsweek*:

> Aggressive government marketing of gambling gives a legitimizing imprimatur to the pursuit of wealth without work. . . . Gambling is debased speculation, a craving for sudden wealth unconnected with investment that might make society more productive. . . . Lotteries—skill-less gambling; gambling for the lazy—are booming at a time when the nation's productivity, competitiveness, savings rate, and academic performance are poor."[5] (There will be more about the down side of gambling in Chapter 5.)

## Big Business

Lotteries are simple to understand. States sell tickets and bettors choose the numbers they think will come up in a drawing. Some lotteries offer "scratchers." Players scratch off a latex covering to find out what is beneath. Matching three numbers or beating a poker hand or 21 hand, means you win something—another scratcher, $5, $10, or as much as $25,000.

States have started to pool payouts to drum up

42

business, and a new generation of lottery products guarantees even more revenue. The most recent lottery game innovation is the video lottery terminal (VLT), which is similar to a video arcade game. Unlike Pac-Man, VLTs let you choose from a variety of games—poker, blackjack, keno, and bingo. (More on these casino games later in this chapter.)

VLTs are identical to casino slot machines, except that VLTs print out a receipt redeemable for cash when you win, and slots pay out winnings in cash. VLTs are a lucrative new source of lottery revenue for states. By some estimates VLTs bring in five to ten times *more* than conventional lotteries. When the state of South Dakota introduced VLTs in 1992, lottery revenues jumped more than *$100 million.*

The companies that make lottery equipment also make a lot of money. A single VLT costs $5,000. Some estimates show the legal market for VLT production could top $1.5 billion. That doesn't count illegal VLTs in operation, which could add another $750 million to manufacturers' coffers.[6] (See more about illegal gambling in Chapter 5.)

The advertising industry is another beneficiary of lotteries. Historically, lottery sales die down after they are introduced. To counter the slack, lotteries advertise to the tune of almost $300 million per year, making lotteries one of the top fifty advertisers in the United States.

Lottery tickets are bought on impulse, like gum and cigarettes, so convenience stores are given colorful banners to catch patrons' attention. The stores also place lottery tickets near cigarettes and candy bars to lure customers into buying a ticket before they leave with their other purchases.

## A National Lottery?

It looks as if the federal government may step into the lottery business as a means of making up the budget deficit. As Paul Magnusson wrote in *Business Week,* "Alone among major revenue raisers . . . lotteries pass the White House 'duck' test: A lottery doesn't look, walk, or sound like a tax."[7] Bettors could place bets at computer terminals in post offices or could allocate part of their tax refund to the federal lottery. "If the federal government could keep 50% of the receipts—$7.6 billion of $19 billion, say—that approximates a tax of $5 to $7.50 per barrel on imported petroleum. Or a gasoline tax hike of ten cents a gallon."[8]

A national lottery would have opposition from both legislators and voters. The states want to protect their lottery revenue, and citizens worry about the deleterious affects of gambling on Americans and society. According to *Advertising Age,* lotteries ". . . glorify get-rich-quick schemes, and that's bad public policy."[9]

Lotteries also encourage gambling. Surveys show that one-fourth of the people who otherwise don't gamble at all, purchase lottery tickets.[10] VLTs, in particular, are highly addictive, especially for young people. They have been called a "compulsive gambler's dream."[11]

Just fifty years ago, a lottery initiative would never have passed in any state. Today, thirty-four states have legalized lotteries, and the number is growing each year. A national lottery in the future may not be too far-fetched.

## Casinos

While gambling means different things to different people, for many people it means casinos. And the granddaddy of all casino cities is Las Vegas, Nevada.[12]

Las Vegas rises from the desert like a neon oasis. More than twenty million people visit Las Vegas each year. They leave behind $10 billion, spent on sightseeing, golf, amusement parks, shopping, meals, entertainment, and of course, gambling.

Casinos weren't the first gambling activity to occur in the Las Vegas area. For hundreds of years, the Las Vegas Paiute Indians played a sticks-and-bones game. Two players started the game with five sticks each. One player hid one of two bones—a plain bleached bone and a black-banded bone—in each hand. If the other player guessed in which hand which bones were hidden, that player would win a stick. The two players then changed places. The player with the most sticks won the game.

Until the 1940s Las Vegas wasn't much more than a blip in the eastern edge of the Mojave Desert. Its reputation centered around being one of the hottest, driest cities in the United States. Then in 1946 gangster Bugsy Siegel opened the Flamingo casino. Las Vegas was never the same.

Unlike the Bugsy portrayed in movies, the real Bugsy Siegel was a vicious thug who had committed just about every major crime in the book: extortion, hijacking, narcotics, rape, and murder. He raised $1 million for the Flamingo casino from his mob bosses, but when the final bill for the casino and hotel reached $5 million, his financial backers became very nervous. They wanted to see a good return on this investment. Unfortunately for Bugsy, when the Flamingo opened, it flopped and soon closed. The

The Las Vegas Strip at night comes alive with superstar entertainment, production show spectaculars, and casino action.

failure sealed Bugsy's fate. His "business partners" had him killed.

New management took over the Flamingo, and the casino reopened, this time successfully. Over the next ten years, casinos and hotels blossomed, Las Vegas grew as a gambling center, and more criminals moved in to get their share of casino profits. Las Vegas gained a new reputation—this time as a haven for the underworld.

According to the book *Las Vegas* by Deke Castleman, "Hustlers, scam artists, smalltime hoods, prostitutes, thieves, degenerates, and compulsive gamblers, boomtowners, tradesmen, and tourists flooded the place. . . . Clearly, Las Vegas had been declared 'open territory' by the Mafia, meaning that any [crime] family with the inclination could operate there, without fear of territorial reprisals."[13]

In 1950 U.S. Senator Estes Kefauver led the Committee to Investigate Organized Crime. The committee held hearings in Las Vegas and established a link between the casinos and gangsters from New York, Chicago, Cleveland, and California. In 1955, the state of Nevada created the Gaming Control Board to license and police the casinos. By the 1960s, the state legislature forced the State Gaming Commission to tighten control over casinos. Then-U.S. Attorney General Robert Kennedy turned on the heat, and the media began to expose the criminal element that lurked beneath the Las Vegas glitter.

Over the next decade Las Vegas grew by leaps and

bounds. Major hotels and casinos added ten thousand rooms, showrooms, lounges, and big-name entertainment. Meanwhile the Gaming Commission and Control Board tightened licensing and revenue reporting. The FBI and IRS moved in along with the Department of Labor and Bureau of Narcotics to clean up the gangster element. Then came Howard Hughes, a legitimate, but reclusive, billionaire business mogul. He bought casinos and hotels all over town and began legitimizing the gambling business. Suddenly casinos were being run by top-notch business people with graduate degrees in all areas of business. The mob was replaced by MBAs.

Las Vegas became respectable. Today the town has a new reputation as a major tourist destination and is one of the fastest growing cities in the United States.

## Where the Money Comes From

The billions of dollars dropped at casinos each year by gamblers is left at a variety of games.[14] For all games, except roulette, gamblers use United States currency and coins, casino dollars, or casino chips. Casino dollars are similar to silver dollars. Chips are tokens that are assigned different face values starting with $1. Casino dollars and chips can only be used in the casino that issues them.

The odds always favor the casino, or the "house." Over the long term, most people always lose more than they win. Here's an overview of the most popular casino games.

This twenty-foot high statue of Caesar is at the entrance to Caesar's Palace, Las Vegas. Caesar's Palace is one of Las Vegas's most lavish hotel/casinos. The large dome in the background is the roof of the Omnimax Theatre, which shows 70mm movies in the round.

**Craps.** The craps table is surrounded by a rim to make sure that the dice don't leave the table surface. The table itself is marked with the various kinds of bets possible. When the dice are thrown, the number may be an immediate winner or loser.

**Keno.** Keno comes from China, and has been played for about three thousand years. Starting with the Gold Rush, the game arrived in the United States with the waves of Chinese immigrants.

Keno is a lottery-type game. A large clear bubble holds white balls, each of which has a number from one to 80 written on it. During play, the balls are stirred upward with an air jet. Then twenty of them drop randomly from the bubble, one at a time. The numbers on the balls are the winning numbers for that play. Before the balls are dropped, bettors pick the numbers that they think will drop, choosing from one to twenty.

Can you win at keno? The odds of choosing eight out of eight numbers are 230,114 to 1. The odds of hitting twelve out of twelve numbers are 500 million to 1.

**Poker.** Poker is legal in many states that don't allow casino gambling. In fact, many people sit down at someone's home for a friendly poker game with their buddies on a weekly basis.

Poker is a game of skill. Players compete against each other, not the casino. The casino gets its money by taking 10 percent of the pot—the money gambled by each player in the game.

There are many varieties of poker. Players are dealt

Raking in the take in a poker game.

five cards and discard as many as they want. Replacement cards are dealt. Certain combinations of cards beat other combinations. For example, two pairs beat one pair. Three of a kind beats two pairs.

The goal is to get one of several winning hands. Certain hands outrank others, for example, three aces outranks three queens. All through the process of dealing, discarding, and replacing cards, each player places bets that his hand will be the winning one. The player with the winning hand gets the pot, less the percentage for the casino.

**Race and sports betting.** Sports and race wagering is big business in casinos, and adds about $40 million per year to casino coffers.

Casinos spend millions of dollars on computerized sports betting that uses satellite dishes to beam in games from across the nation on giant screens in casino race and sports lounges. Race and sports betting offer a supermarket of sports gambling in one location. You can wager on just about any major sports event around the country, from horse racing at Bay Meadows in California to the Super Bowl in Miami to a college football game in Boston.

Sports betting is the most popular gambling activity in America, although casinos take in only a fraction of all money bet on racing and sports activities. More than $1 billion per year is bet legally at casinos; more than $26 billion is bet illegally.

**Roulette.** Roulette is played at a table marked with a grid of numbers from 1 to 36, plus 0 and 00, and a

Sports betting is a popular casino game.

wheel with black and red slots that correspond to the numbers on the grid. For the play, the wheel is spun and the ball is released in a direction opposite to the spinning wheel.

Before the ball is released, betters place wagers on which number they think the ball will land, on whether the number will be red or black, where in the sequence of 1 to 36 it will fall, or whether the number will be odd or even.

After the ball spins and bounces around on the wheel, it lands in a slot. The number corresponding to the slot is the winning number. A better who has placed a wager on the winning number, color, or sequence wins. Of course, all the others lose.

**Slots.** This is the only casino game where you can win a million dollars or more. Slots from several casinos across the state are connected by telephone modem. Called "progressive" slots, they allow casinos to pool payouts, so that winners can hit jackpots worth millions of dollars. If this sounds like a good deal, keep in mind that slots are also called one-armed bandits because they take your money and rarely pay off big time.

Casinos advertise a slot return. The higher the return, the more money the casino pays out. However, the casino always keeps a portion of every one dollar. For example, when a casino advertises a "94 percent return" on the slots, they mean that for every $100 bet, $94 is paid out. In this case the casino keeps 6 percent of all the money fed into its slots.

Think about it. If your friend asked you to give her $1 in exchange for 94 cents, would you do it? Of course not. You would lose six cents on the deal. Yet, why do millions of people do it when the odds against winning are so high?

According to Ann Magnuson, writing in *Bazaar* magazine, ". . . It's that small glimmer of hope, that burning ember of naiveté—the same misguided optimism that continually had Charlie Brown duped into believing that Lucy would not pull the football away just as he was going to kick it—that drives us to put one more quarter in the slot machine and hopefully change our lives forever."[15]

Originally slots were mechanical. You dropped in a single coin, pulled the handle, and three wheels decorated with pictures of fruit—oranges, watermelons, and cherries—spun. The goal was to have the same fruit line up three across. If they didn't line up, or if you got a lemon on a reel, you lost.

A modern progressive slot machine is linked to slots in casinos around the state in order to pay multimillion-dollar payoffs.

Today, slots are computerized. Often progressive slot machines have four reels with twenty-five possible stops on each wheel. With this kind of machine, the odds of winning a million-dollar jackpot are 9.77 million to 1.

**21.** 21 is a game that requires thought and decision-making. The house odds change with each hand, and the game requires the most skill of all the casino games. As a result, it is the only casino game where the bettor can beat the house odds. It's also one of the most popular casino games. Gamblers spend one-third of their time at the 21 tables. The *minimum* bet required to play, which varies from table to table, starts at $1 or $2 per hand.

Each card has a point value. An ace counts as 1 or 11, face cards are 10, and all other cards are counted at face value. The player plays against the casino or house. The dealer gives each player two cards, and the goal is to come as close as possible to a total of 21 without going over. Players can have as many extra cards as they want as long as they don't go over 21. The casino keeps between 18 and 19 percent of all money bet at 21 tables.

## Odds Always Favor the House

Most of the money that flows into casinos stays in casino coffers.[16] Fewer than 1 percent of gamblers wins in the long run. Every game is designed so that the house always has an edge.

Take roulette as an example. With thirty eight numbers on the wheel (1 through 36, plus 0 and 00),

# Las Vegas Fast Facts

♣More than twenty one million people visit Las Vegas each year.[17]

♠90 percent of all visitors to Las Vegas gamble an average of 4.9 hours a day.

♣The average dollar slot machine earns more than $48,000 per year.

♠Casino dice are accurate to within 1/10,000th of an inch. That's like splitting a hair on your head ten times.

♣The term "lemon" for a bad piece of merchandise originated from slot machines. If you got a lemon on a slot reel, you automatically lost.

♠The eighteen-story neon sign at the Stardust is the brightest sign in Las Vegas—with forty thousand lights, thirty miles of wiring, and thirty-eight tons of steel, paint, and concrete.

the payoff should be 38 to 1. But it isn't. The payoff is 35 to 1. This means that if you bet $1 and your number comes up, you don't get $38, you get $35.

Casinos are designed to keep you playing. There are no clocks, and doors are far apart. The noise level is controlled to sound exciting. Liquor is offered free to any player who wants a drink. Keno runners wander through the restaurants so bettors can play Keno while you eat. Cash machines are handy, so bettors can tap into their checking or savings accounts when they've lost their money. Moving sidewalks effortlessly carry bettors into the casino and leave them at the casino entrance to the games where the action is. They have to walk out—often walking for blocks before they hit the sidewalk.

## Where Casinos Are Headed

Today Las Vegas faces competition from lotteries and casinos across the United States and needs new ways of marketing itself to visitors. As Barney Vinson described in *Las Vegas Behind the Tables:*

> The hotel owners huddled with their department heads, and the public accountants huddled with their computers. The casinos began more aggressive marketing programs, aimed at recapturing the magic that had always given Las Vegas that little edge over everybody else. Conventions were stepped up, along with special events like golf tournaments, professional boxing matches, blackjack tourneys, celebrity poker games, and rodeos. . . . All of it was a desperate gamble by a desperate city. . . . Somehow the gamble paid off.[18]

Today, casinos and gambling are only one part of the tourist scene in Las Vegas. Las Vegas always drew big-name entertainers to its showrooms; today the casinos offer elaborate spectacles. You can see *Starlight Express* at the Las Vegas Hilton; Siegfried and Roy's magic extravaganza, complete with white tigers and a disappearing elephant at The Mirage; and the sinking of a replica of the Titanic at Bally's.

The business of casinos is no longer just gambling.

Rare white tigers greet visitors at the white tiger habitat in the Mirage Hotel and Casino, Las Vegas.

Las Vegas now claims to offer entertainment for the whole family, although in many cases, the entertainment seems to just cover the real business of Las Vegas—which is gambling.

The public relations campaign to turn Las Vegas into a "family" destination seems to be working. Couples who once avoided Las Vegas because there was nothing there for their kids, are being lured to the desert town by mega-resorts and theme parks that cater to the entire family:

- MGM Grand Hotel has created a Disneyland-sized theme park behind its five thousand-room hotel and casino.

- Treasure Island hotel and casino stages a life-sized sea battle between a pirate ship and navy clipper each hour.

- Luxor is a twenty-nine-million cubic foot pyramid complete with a Nile "river," wild rides, and a replica of King Tut's tomb.

- Circus Circus puts on real circus acts above the casino floor, and offers kids an area complete with carnival games and Grand Slam Canyon, a five-acre amusement part with a roller coaster.

- The Mirage greets visitors with an erupting volcano outside its doors, and inside, rare white tigers roam in a special tiger grotto.

Will this shift of emphasis from gambling to family activities make a difference? Only time can tell. Meanwhile Las Vegas must compete with the spread of legal casino gambling across the United States.

*Cards are war, in disguise of a sport.*

–Charles Lamb, "Mrs. Battle's Opinions on Whist,"
Essays of Elia, 1823

# Casino Craze Hits America

For years Nevada was the only state that allowed gambling. Visitors pumped big bucks into the casinos, some of which ended up in state coffers as casinos paid taxes on their take. Because Nevada earns so much revenue from casino taxes, it doesn't have to tax individuals. Nevada residents pay no personal income tax or estate taxes.[1] Then came Atlantic City, New Jersey, and the door to national casino gambling was kicked open.

## Atlantic City

In the early 1970s city officials in Atlantic City began looking at casino gaming as a way to rejuvenate their depressed economy and lower their high unemployment. The belief was that casinos would create jobs, increase the tax base, raise much-needed revenue, and encourage tourism. According to *The Atlantic City Gamble,* "Gambling was billed as a sort of magic bullet that would spur growth and lower unemployment, transforming a blighted city in the process."[2]

Proponents of casino gambling staged a huge campaign to convince New Jersey voters to approve a gaming initiative. David Spanier in *Easy Money* reported, "The supporters of gambling always have a lot more money to play with than the opponents. More than that, some of the supporters of gambling in Atlantic City came from very shady backgrounds."[3]

At the turn of the century Atlantic City was a glittering popular resort town. By 1978 when the first casino opened, it had degenerated into a seedy broken-down shadow of its former self. Gambling has created twenty-nine thousand jobs, lures more than thirty million visitors each year, and has provided more than $3 billion to the state in gaming taxes, but very few benefits have come to Atlantic City itself. Unemployment, crime, and poverty are just about what they were in 1978. "Atlantic City has not profited from the arrival of casinos," Spanier wrote. "[It] is a dump . . . a string of high-rise casinos in a wasteland of non-development . . . eleven casinos along the boardwalk and nothing else . . . apart from a rising crime rate. . . . Employees who staff the casinos mostly come from out of town: they have to because there is no new housing, no schools, no amenities of any kind."[4]

The Wizard welcomes visitors to the Excalibur Hotel and Casino, Las Vegas.

There are plans to pull the city out of its mire by building a $500-million boardwalk with attractions and a casino-free hotel. Whether it succeeds or not is another gamble the city is taking.

## Native American Reservations

Since Atlantic City opened its doors to casinos, gambling fever has spread across the United States.[5] As stated before, only two states—Hawaii and Utah—prohibit gambling. The movement started in 1988 when voters in South Dakota allowed the remote mining town of Deadwood to open a casino, and the Iowa legislature approved casino gambling on riverboats. Other states began approving their own casinos in competition. Today, riverboat casinos ply the Mississippi and almost two hundred Native American communities operate casinos or other types of gambling activities on reservations.

One of the most important events for gambling in 1988 was the passage of the Indian Gaming Regulatory Act (IGRA). The IGRA allows tribes to offer gambling activities that are permitted within their state.

Congress passed the act in response to a 1987 Supreme Court decision, *Cabazon* v. *the State of California.* As Harvey Shapiro described the situation in the publication *Hemispheres:*

> [The Supreme Court] decision required states with legal gambling activities to give Indian reservations an equal right to operate commercial gambling on tribal land. Because Indian lands are sovereignties— exempt from most state controls and taxes—states

were left with uncertain authority over Indian gambling within their borders. . . . IGRA . . . ignited an explosion of Vegas-style casinos on reservations. . . . Dozens of reservation communities have thus far signed agreements with industry stars like Harrah's and Circus Circus to lure gamblers to tribal casinos.[6]

Gambling is seen as a boon to Native American communities, where unemployment and suicide are double the national average and alcoholism is seven times worse. According to *The New York Times,* leaders in these communities across the nation "see more cause for optimism now than at any other time in generations, perhaps even since whites arrived. But the driving force behind these new hopes lies with gambling, what some have called 'the new buffalo money.'"[7] For example, the Mystic Lake Casino on the Shakopee Mdewekantan [sic] Reservation in Minnesota paid each of the tribe's two hundred members more than $400,000 from gambling revenues in 1993. In 1992, the Colorado Utes used revenue from gambling to purchase gas fields to start their own profitable drilling company. The California Sycuan band of Mission Indians took their gambling revenues to construct new houses for each member and opened new fire and police stations.

In 1992, the take from Native American casinos hit $1.5 billion. This money is financing new schools, housing, roads, and hospitals. It is also making Native American communities independent of government aid for the first time in their long and painful association with whites. According to an article in *The New*

Animated life-size dinosaurs hiss and roar as visitors explore the $90-million Grand Slam Canyon at Circus Circus hotel/casino on the Las Vegas Strip. The five-acre climate controlled Adventuredome houses the only double loop, double corkscrew indoor roller coaster in the United States.

*York Times,* "After more than a century of federal policies that ranged from extermination to assimilation, Indian nations have lately gained a greater degree of self-determination . . . spelled out in the Supreme Court ruling in 1987 that liberated tribes, as sovereign nations, from most state gambling regulations."[8]

A prime example of a successful reservation casino is Foxwoods. It is the largest Native American casino in the nation and is located on the Mashantucket Pequot Reservation in Connecticut. Since Foxwoods opened in 1992, attendance has averaged fifteen to twenty thousand on weekdays and twenty to thirty thousand on weekends. People wait in lines to play slot machines and take turns at 21 tables. Foxwoods has been so successful that it is adding more gaming areas, shops, and restaurants. It is now one of the largest casino complexes in the world. Because Foxwoods is a private tribal business, it doesn't have to disclose its earnings. Experts guess that it takes in as much as $800 million a year.  Has this income allowed Foxwoods to bring benefits to the area?

It's too soon to tell, but in 1992 visitors left behind $6 million spent on local nongambling attractions. Regional tourist boards believe that the boost in tourism due to Foxwoods will continue to pour much needed money into the area.  There are other benefits, too. The Pequots have broken ground on a museum of Native American culture. And they plan a theme park in conjunction with the Chinese government in partnership with a Malaysian investor, who originally helped finance Foxwoods.

Not everyone is happy with the success of Foxwoods. Local residents complain about traffic. Many residents are concerned that the Pequots want to add local land to the reservation, thus reducing property tax rolls. Critics also believe that the Native American casinos have an unfair advantage over other casinos because Native American casinos are exempt from much of the regulation that governs nonreservation casinos.

Not all Native Americans support the rise of casinos and gambling. In one case opposition resulted in bloodshed.[9] The Mohawk reservation of Akwesasne spreads across both the northern United States and southern Canada at the Raquette, Grass, St. Regis, and St. Lawrence rivers. Once the tribe was united; now, it is divided over the issue of casinos.

A group called the Warriors saw how gambling was proving to be an economic salvation for other tribes. They believed that the Mohawks could benefit from a casino. Lands for farming and waterways for fishing were too polluted to be profitable; businesses had been tried and died in the past. So maybe gambling would lure visitors to the reservation and pump much needed revenue into the tribal economy.

The Antis, on the other hand, were tribal elders who opposed gambling as immoral and a violation of the Mohawk way. They feared that allowing gambling on the reservation would open the door to organized crime and drugs. One of the men financing the casino had been linked to organized crime and had been denied a gaming license in Nevada, where illegal connections are carefully investigated. Despite the conflict, a bingo palace and an illegal casino opened.

The "war" between the Warriors and Antis escalated with beatings, driveby shootings, and arson. The Antis created permanent barricades from logs and barrels to cut off the highway and prevented access to the bingo palace and the casino. They begged federal and state authorities to close the casino.

The Warriors, many of whom had invested in the casino, assaulted the roadblock on April 24, 1990, wielding baseball bats and lead pipes. Guns fired, the roadblocks fell, and two thousand Antis fled.

The fighting that escalated among the Warriors and the Antis that remained centered around a single house manned by three Antis brothers—Davey, Doug, and Dean George—their brother-in-law, and a cousin.

As author Daniel D'Ambrosio described the tense situation:

> The Warriors dug in and kept their sights on this last vestige of opposition. There was scattered gunfire, especially at night, and outbursts of violence, as when Davey set a Warrior car on fire. During the day, the Antis would ferry in food and occasionally weapons to the Georges. Some of them would stay. By the fourth day, there were eleven men in the house. . . . On the final night of the standoff, the gunfire began around nine-thirty and went on almost continuously until eight the next morning.[10]

Five thousand rounds were fired. Two men died. Authorities arrested Doug George, then released him. The bingo hall and casino were closed. The deaths of the two men have not been investigated, and despite the efforts of the Antis, legal gambling is coming to Akwesasne. Two of the three elected chiefs of the American Mohawk Tribal Council have signed an agreement to open a legal casino with a well-known casino contractor.

## Do Casinos Pay Off?

Economic data seem to indicate that when casinos spring up, spending on other forms of entertainment such as bowling, tennis, and billiards, declines.[11] In some states, gambling has benefited local economies. For example, since opening its casinos, Biloxi, Mississippi, has reduced unemployment in the casino area by 3.7 percent, and forty-seven thousand people work for the casinos.

On the other side of the coin, *The Wall Street Journal* stated:

> In the pell-mell rush, seeds of potential problems are being planted. Issues such as compulsive gambling and underage gambling are mostly ignored. Of the 48 states that allow some form of wagering, Texas is nearly alone in allocating a small percentage of gaming revenue to research into related social problems. And issues such as gambling attracting crime and corruption continue to hover on the fringes of public debate like an uninvited party guest.[12]

Some areas have seen local businesses adversely affected by gambling. Small restaurants and hotels cannot compete with big casinos. In Atlantic City, one hundred of the city's two hundred and fifty restaurants have closed since the casinos opened and retail business has dropped one-third. In Biloxi, there are four new pawnshops, each stocked with wedding and engagement rings left behind by gamblers, some on their

The Mirage and Treasure Island hotels/casinos in Las Vegas cater to both gamblers and non-gamblers by offering state of the art casino games and spectacular entertainment for the entire family.

honeymoons. Five chapters of Gamblers Anonymous have opened to help compulsive gamblers. (There will be more about the downside of gambling in Chapter 5.)

The casinos are also affecting the environment. In March 1994 in Biloxi, "every casino . . . was found to be violating sewage discharge laws. Illegal grease and oil dumping were clogging lines and creating noxious fumes."[13]

Competition is also a concern. The prosperous Indian casino run by the Omaha tribe in Nebraska was dealt a blow to its income when Iowa approved a casino nearby. And California is cutting into Nevada's gambling business.

# Fast Facts About the Hottest Casino States

As of year-end 1993:[14]

| STATE | No. OF CASINOS | REVENUE |
|---|---|---|
| Nevada | 98 | $6.22 billion |
| New Jersey | 12 | $3.3 billion |
| Mississippi | 11 | $782.5 million |
| Illinois | 5 | $605.9 million |
| Colorado | 37 | $257.2 million |
| South Dakota | 84 | $43.5 million |
| Iowa | 2 | $41.6 million |

California's constitution prohibits casinos and slot machines. In 1993, however, a federal judge ruled that Indians could offer both slot machines and casino gambling on reservations because the California lottery offered a similar form of gambling. Under IGRA, California's Native Americans had the right to offer this kind of gaming on reservation land. The Agua Caliente band of Cahuilla Indians, which owns much of the land around posh Palm Springs, plans to build a $20-million casino and shopping mall with Caesars World of Las Vegas. More and more big-time casino operators from Nevada are forming liaisons with Indian tribes to ensure that they get a piece of the take.

There are three hundred legal casinos in the United States, and more are coming. Harrah's plans to open the world's largest casino in New Orleans next year. Detroit may be the first major city to have casino gambling, as a result of a referendum passed late last summer. Chicago is also exploring putting a casino in the middle of town.

About 70 percent of the U.S. population lives within three hundred miles of a casino; this number will increase to 95 percent by the turn of the century. According to *The New York Times,* in 1993, "More Americans went to casinos than to major league ball parks."[15] They spent more than $330 billion on gambling activities. Indian gambling alone is expected to grow $500 million a year.

The gambling phenomenon is going international. England has a lottery—its first since 1826—and bingo halls are booming. Moscow has opened several casinos, and more than forty casinos have opened in the Czech Republic since its independence. Lebanese citizens risked getting shot to visit casinos in the war zone of West Beirut. Peru now permits casino gambling, and Greece and China both have plans to open casinos.

*The Wall Street Journal* also says, "The financial markets also have an increased stake in gambling mania. Wall Street's betting fever rages on, with the number of gambling-related stocks—from riverboat operators to equipment manufacturers—leaping to more than 50 from just 20 two years ago."[16]

Where will it end? No one knows. One day you may be able to gamble from the comfort of your living room. A Florida inventor recently received a patent that can allow people to legally bet on televised game shows, sporting events, and beauty pageants. Making it so easy to gamble may not be good. People who are problem or compulsive gamblers may find it even more difficult to avoid gambling activities that are available in their own living room.

*True luck consists not in holding the best of the cards at the table; Luckiest he who knows just when to rise and go home.*

–John Jay, *Distichs* [sic], 1871.

# 5

# The Downside of Gambling

Many teens come from families where one or both parents are compulsive gamblers.[1] They have negative role models and little support for *not* gambling. The gambling parent may either indulge the child or ignore him or her. Teens who live with gambling parents realize that no matter what they do, gambling will always be more important than they are. They may feel that something is wrong with them, that—in some way—they are responsible for the parent's gambling. Some teens may identify with the exciting aspects of gambling and begin gambling themselves to overcome the pain of being ignored.

Compulsive gamblers are often irritable and moody. They can cut someone in half with their sarcasm. And often they may become verbally and physically abusive, especially if they are losing. The gambling parent may ask teens to lie to protect him or her, or may borrow the teen's money to finance gambling activities. Often teens find themselves in the middle of warring parents, with the nongambling parent pitting the children against the gambling parent. In this type of situation, teens may feel confused and worried. They may also experience shame, a feeling that they are bad for a reason they can't identify. Children of gamblers often feel depressed and anxious. They may either act as the parents of the parent, or may act out their feelings by rebelling and creating problems at home or school.

Parental gambling can wreck havoc on a family's finances. Often money that should go to pay bills is spent at the track, casino, or on lottery tickets. Some families must file bankruptcy. Others struggle from paycheck to paycheck to make ends meet. This affects a teen's relationship with money, causing some teens to become spendthrifts; others to hoard money. Many lie to cover up the family's financial difficulties and protect themselves from outsiders discovering the parent's addiction.

Sometimes a sibling has a gambling problem. How a teen reacts to a brother or sister with a gambling problem depends on the kind of relationship the two have. Teens in this position often face the difficult problem of having to tell parents about the gambling teen. In addition, parents may have to devote so much attention to the gambling teen, other family members feel neglected and less important.

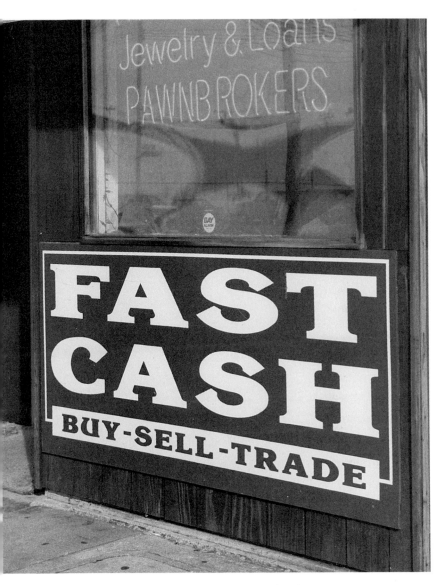

Gambers sometimes pawn valuables to get their betting money.

Compulsive gambling can destroy families and haunt the lives of family members for years. It causes family disruption, neglected or abused children, divorce, impoverishment, and/or mental breakdown. Actress Debbie Reynolds was married to two compulsive gamblers who lost all their own money and hers, too. Baseball player Pete Rose ruined his career and his life gambling illegally. Basketball player Michael Jordan is rumored to have lost $1 million to a golf buddy while betting on the links.

As *Newsweek* reported, "But the problem with gambling in America isn't really with fabulously wealthy athletes wagering $10,000 on a putt; it's with ordinary people betting money they can't afford on games that exploit their naiveté and greed. . . . That money is coming from somewhere: their paycheck, savings accounts, money they borrow. Some of it is stolen."[2]

## Can Gamblers Be Helped?

Very few states have programs for teen gamblers. Few teens realize how addictive gambling—especially lotteries and casino gambling—can become. According to experts, gambling is as addictive as alcohol and drugs.

Recovery groups for teens usually focus on alcohol and drug abuse, not gambling. Some Gamblers Anonymous groups are attended solely by adults with whom the teen feels he or she has little in common. In some cases, the only therapy available to compulsive teen gamblers is group therapy with a psychologist, psychiatrist, or social welfare counselor. New programs are being developed; ironically, many are being funded with state revenues obtained from gambling sources. According to Dr. Durand Jacobs, "Little will change until society begins to view teenage gambling with the same alarm directed at drugs and alcohol. Gambling is the addiction of the 90s."[3]

Some experts believe that compulsive gamblers are incurable. Others are more optimistic. The gambler needs help getting to the heart of the problem and finding out why he or she is addicted to this destructive activity.

According to the Council on Compulsive Gambling of New Jersey:

> Help can come only if the observant parent, husband or wife, relative or employer recognizes that a loved and valued person is suffering from a disease for which he is no more responsible than one who is congenitally blind. Indeed, the very nature of the disease is a kind of blindness which prevents the gambler from seeing his actions as pathological symptoms. For this reason, few compulsive gamblers can recover without the help of others. The gambler must be motivated in every way possible to realize the seriousness of the disease in order to seek help. There is no doubt that compulsive gambling can be treated.[4]

Gamblers Anonymous helps gamblers to realize that they have no control over gambling. The cure is to quit gambling entirely. The gambler can get help putting together a repayment schedule for debts, and follows a twelve-step program based on the program originally created for Alcoholics Anonymous. Compulsive gamblers often attend one meeting a day, or sometimes more than one, as they try to overcome their addiction. The compulsion is something they fight every day. Often, when the gambler quits, he or she experiences symptoms of withdrawal similar to narcotics withdrawal. Fellow members of Gamblers Anonymous can help someone through this difficult time. Generally, recovered gamblers continue to attend weekly meetings to help support their recovery.

With only 600 Gamblers Anonymous chapters nationwide, people often must travel great distances to attend meetings. Only about 20 public and private treatment centers for gambling exist and their waiting lists are long. This makes it difficult for the recovered gambler to find the support he or she needs to keep from placing a bet.

On the bright side, a new law in Iowa requires that one percent of all lottery revenues go to public awareness programs and treatment. New Jersey requires that lottery locations post signs with the toll-free number of the National Council on Compulsive Gambling. Other states are looking into similar types of requirements.

## Animal Rights

People aren't the only ones who suffer from gambling. Some games involving animals are common to certain cultures and are subjects of gambling. In the United States, rodeos, horse racing, and greyhound racing are big businesses. Then, there are illegal games involving animals such as cockfighting and pit bull fights. In many cases, the animals used in these "sports" often live painful, restricted lives that end in violence and death. Let's look at two sports involving animal rights—both are subjects of heavy gambling—cockfighting and greyhound racing.

## Cockfighting

While cockfighting was a popular activity in the United States during the Revolutionary period, today only six states allow cockfighting.[5]

Cocks fight with each other naturally to establish a territory or secure a mate. However, owners raise their birds to do battle. The cocks are bred for maximum aggressiveness and are fed high-protein food and drugs. It can cost more than $6,000 a year just to feed a game cock, so owners seek to recoup their costs and earn money through the fights, which can have pots of $20,000 or more.

Cockfighting is a bloody, violent sport. The owners augment the cocks' natural spurs with metal ones attached to the back of the bird's left leg. The false spur is from 2.54 centimeters (1 inch) to 7.62 centimeters (3 inches) long. Americans use a sickle shaped blade; Mexicans prefer a long straight blade; Cajuns use a sharpened tortoise-shell pike. When two or more birds have been fitted with spurs, they are placed in a pit to fight to the death.

A fight can last up to half an hour as the birds mutilate each other with their false razor-sharp spurs. Injuries run the gamut from punctured lungs to pierced eyes, and broken bones. Exhausted and injured birds are not rescued. The fight continues until one

Race horses often suffer physical damage and sometimes death.

animal is dead or too injured to continue fighting, at which time it is either put to death or tossed aside to die slowly and painfully. Here's how a reporter for *The Economist* magazine described a cockfight:

> As the two handlers step into the pit. . . . The crowd erupts in a frenzy of betting. You shout out a . . . wager . . . and look to find someone who will take up the other side of the bet. The handlers sway rhythmically three times towards each other to get the birds mad. They then set the birds on the ground behind two lines drawn in the cockpit's sand. The roosters' hackles rise and they fly at . . . each other, pecking at necks and stabbing at breasts, all in a blur of feathers. . . . Although the victor will often live to fight another day, the loser has had it. The . . . favoured way to kill the gamecock is to tread on its head and pull it up by

the legs. . . . You then throw the warm bird into the dustbins at the back of the club, along with the beer cans.[6]

Law enforcement agencies have documented the connection between cockfighting and drugs. Drug Enforcement Administration (DEA) agents often attend cockfights because drug dealers are present. Also, illegal betting is normal at cockfights. Thousands of dollars can change hands over a single pot as spectators bet on the cocks. Because so much money is involved, many gamblers carry guns and other weapons for protection.

Other types of criminal activity have been associated with cockfighting. In Texas, a woman was gang raped at a cockfight. Law enforcement agencies have also connected a number of murders to cockfighting.

Children often attend cockfights, and may even participate. This can lead to an insensitivity to animal suffering and a belief that criminal activity is acceptable. One drug agent undercover at a cockfight in Ohio was offered a $150 wager by a nine-year-old.

## Greyhound Racing

Once greyhounds were used as hunting dogs, to help put food on the table.[7] Today, dog racing is legal in nineteen states; but despite this, it is one of society's crueler sports. According to experts, half of the greyhounds bred for racing are killed by gunshot or a blow to the head before they reach the race track. According to estimates, forty thousand puppies and adolescent dogs die in this preliminary cut—usually the runts, the slow starters, and stubborn hounds.

The life of the racing dog is hard. Top-winning dogs are treated better than others while they are winning. When they start to slow down, they are sent to less important tracks. Dogs spend most of their lives in cages, and are muzzled all the time, except for feeding. Some tracks house dogs in insect-infested kennels and feed them cheap, often contaminated, meat.

Most of the survivors who make it to the track have only death to look forward to. As dogs become lame or injured, or if their speed slows, or when they stop winning, they are destroyed by gunshot or bludgeoning. The unlucky ones are sent to research labs. The death toll is estimated to be another thirty thousand dogs a year. About seventy thousand dogs a year are destroyed for this "sport."

Greyhounds aren't the only animals to suffer. In order to encourage the dogs to race, they are trained with live lures—small animals such as rabbits, chickens, guinea pigs, and even kittens.

The rabbit or other small animal is attached to a whirligig, a mechanical contraption that goes around the track very fast. The dogs chase the whirligig. Often, the lure's legs are deliberately broken so that its cries of pain draw the dog's attention and encourage it to chase the lure. After the training session, some trainers let the dogs catch the lure and tear it apart to whet the dog's appetite for racing. Experts estimate that one hundred thousand small animals die each year in training exercises.

Animal rescue organizations and citizens are trying

to get trainers to stop using live animals as lures. Other organizations have sprung up to rescue greyhounds and equip them to live with families through animal adoption programs. Only a small fraction of greyhounds are rescued. Most are killed after having spent their lives at race tracks.

Proponents argue that dog racing generates taxes for the states where it is legal. Compared to the state's total tax fund, the amount contributed by greyhound racing is very small. For example, Florida has eighteen of the forty-eight legal greyhound race tracks in the country, but racing generates only .7 percent of Florida's tax revenues. Also the money spent at the track is money that probably would be spent on consumable goods that are also taxed such as CDs, tapes, sporting equipment. These other activities do not involve animal cruelty and would not affect the overall income the state receives from tax revenues.

## Charity Gambling

Each year Americans spend more than $10 billion at games sponsored for the benefit of charitable organizations.[8] This is three times the amount donated to United Way. According to experts, only a fraction of the money spent for charity gambling actually goes to the needy.

Charities, like cash-strapped state governments, have turned to gambling as a way of raising money to compensate for federal and state cutbacks, and reduced private funding. Charity gambling is legal in all states except for Utah, Tennessee, Hawaii, and Arkansas. It helps to fund a variety of worthwhile organizations from Boys and Girls Clubs to assistance for AIDS patients to associations for the mentally and physically challenged. But like most activities associated with gambling, charity gambling has a dark downside. Less than half of the money wagered on charity gambling goes to the charities sponsoring the games. For example, in Florida, only five cents of every dollar spent on charity gambling finds its way to charities. Where does the rest of the money go? About 50 to 80 percent of the take goes to pay off winners. The rest goes to overhead and administrative expenses to run the games. Promoters can get as much as 40 percent of the take.

The games are vulnerable to cheats because they are often run by volunteers who are easily duped by cardsharps. For example, at a charity game in Indiana police discovered that four blackjack players had marked and palmed cards.

Professional criminals associate themselves with charity gambling. They skim cash and charge outrageous fees for administering the games. About 10 percent of all licensed charity games are victims of skimming. For example, police in Maryland discovered that two charity casinos had taken in $5 million, but only reported $1 million, pocketing the $4 million difference.

Some states inadvertently encourage skimming. For example, South Carolina limits the take to $13,000 per day. If a charity gaming business takes in

Two dice showing "snake eyes"—a losing combination in craps.

more than this, it isn't reported. It's skimmed. According to law enforcement officers, three South Carolina men who ran a charity are alleged to have taken in $35 million in charity gambling money over a three-year period, but only turned over $20,000 to the actual charity itself. The case has not yet come to trial.

Crimes involving charity gambling are white-collar crimes. These crimes are time-consuming and expensive to prove and prosecute. Street crime has a much higher priority for law enforcement agencies. Legislators are reluctant to pass laws tightening charity gambling, and they like the tax revenues taken in from the games.

Some states, however, are cracking down. South Dakota requires charity blackjack games to install video cameras to detect cheating. Virginia requires that 6 percent of the take go to the sponsoring charity.

## Crime

Gambling and crime often go together.[9] According to William Webster, former director of the FBI, "I really don't see how one can expect to run legalized gambling anywhere without serious problems—fraudulent tickets, counterfeit lottery processes. Any time organized crime sees an opportunity to put a fix on something, to get an edge on something, it'll be there. And gambling is still the largest source of revenue for organized crime."[10]

Any activity that generates billions of dollars is a likely target for criminals. The relationship between gambling and organized crime is obvious when you identify the states where crime families are located: Nevada, New York, California, Louisiana, and Illinois—all states with legalized gambling activities. Some experts believe that legal gambling encourages illegal gambling. Compulsive gamblers sometimes turn to illegal activities when their money runs out. They then get involved with loan sharks who charge exorbitant fees to borrow money. Loan sharks charge interest of 20 percent per week on loans and use intimidation, beatings, and even murder to collect outstanding debts.

Illegal gambling is popular because no one pays taxes: the winners don't declare their winnings to Uncle Sam, and the proprietors of illegal establishments don't pay taxes on their take. Illegal gambling can also be more convenient than legal gambling. It is easier to place a bet with a bookie than to go to the track.

Once gambling meant crooked casinos with rigged wheels, cardsharp dealers that dealt for the house's advantage, and loaded dice. This is no longer true. Today casinos are heavily regulated and all the games are honest—at the legal casinos. Illegal casinos can be found in every major city in the United States. Unlike their legal counterparts, no regulatory agency oversees these operations and ensures their honesty. Illegal casinos survive by paying local officials or by staying one step ahead of the police. According to Darwin Ortiz in his book *Gambling Scams,* in New York illegal clubs ". . . have enjoyed a windfall as a result of legalization in New Jersey. Atlantic City has created a large new market of gamblers in the New York Area. . . . These joints are not subject to government supervision. [The] only protection against cheating is the club owner's conscience."[11]

Casinos themselves aren't immune from those who try and cheat them. Slot cheats try to force machines to pay off by jamming security devices. The Nevada Gaming Control Board estimates that casinos lose about $10 to $12 million a year to slot cheats.

In addition to illegal casinos, illegal sports betting is big business. According to law enforcement officers, sixty hoodlums in a Chicago suburb have built a $1-billion sports-betting gambling empire. It started when mob bosses moved their families to the suburbs and took their illegal gambling activities—loan sharking, extortion, and sports betting—with them.

In New York a numbers kingpin, Raymond Marquez, was arrested allegedly for doing what the lottery does legally—allow people to bet on which numbers will come up winners. According to allegations, he ran more than forty gambling parlors, disguised as clothing, candy, and variety stores. His clients wagered from ten cents to more than $1,000 a day. He had more than 100 employees, some of whom made more than $17,000 a week on allegedly illegal numbers running. He was captured because he used his fax to get daily reports on gambling activities. The faxes were obtained with a court order, and led to his arrest.

Even seemingly innocent activities such as carnivals can be tainted by illegal activity. Ortiz wrote that,

"Carnival games are one of the most underrated areas of crooked gambling. . . . Some . . . are controlled by organized crime [who] receive 50% of the . . . gross profits."[12]

Businesspeople and tourists are not immune. On street corners in major cities such as New York, people ply an old scam called three-card monte. A man manipulates three cards on a folded newspaper on top of a cardboard carton. The cards are turned face down and mixed up. The bettor guesses where a certain card will end up. The operator uses slight of hand to make sure this card will never be picked; and shills work the crowd to lure in suckers to place bets.

"In the spring and summer, there are about 200 monte mobs in New York City," according to Ortiz.

In three-card monte, a shill—the person who lures others into making wagers—points to where he thinks the winning card will be found.

The three-card monte dealer shows that the shill has won. Dealers and shills dupe players into betting, thinking that they have a chance to win.

"Even the crudest operators take in a couple of hundred dollars a day while the more sophisticated mobs make much more. Individual bets in the $50 to $100 range are quite common."[13]

Even our high schools are not immune, and young people are prime targets for illegal gambling activities. Adult bookies hire teens to take bets inside the school, and they extend credit to young people to encourage them to bet money they don't have and can't afford. When the bettor loses—as is usually the case—the bookie expects to be paid. The teen may turn to crime to pay off gambling debts, then wager more and more, and get in deeper. Most adult compulsive gamblers started their gambling habits this way.

# Epilogue

## Is Gambling Good or Bad?

Is gambling good for us as individuals and as a nation?

Gambling can bring needed revenue to cash-poor states and cities. When these revenues are applied appropriately to improve socioeconomic conditions, gambling can be seen as a boon to society. When gambling revenues aren't used in this way and serve to line the pockets of the greedy and less than honest, then gambling is a bane.

Gambling can create an environment where other kinds of criminal activities breed. Crimes such as prostitution, illegal gambling, drugs, and loan sharking seem to spring up around gambling activities—even legal activities. This causes concern for law enforcement officials. It is one reason why states and gaming control boards require that legal gambling organizations adhere to strict rules and regulations.

Certain kinds of gambling contribute to animal cruelty, and for no redeeming reason. The existence of these types of "games" cannot be justified. They create a belief in participants that animals have no right to be treated with respect, and are merely here for our amusement regardless of what happens to them.

Gambling is here to stay. The United States discovered with the prohibition of alcohol that outlawing certain activities entirely only gives rise to lawlessness, as organized crime moves in to offer the prohibited activities illegally.

Gambling can be an exciting, fun, and entertaining activity. It can also be an obsession that destroys lives and families. The keys to making it work for us rather than against us are:

- Moderation.
- Obedience to and strict enforcement of gambling laws.
- Education about the downside of gambling.
- Assistance for those who are addicted to gambling.
- Safeguards to ensure that public works and other worthy causes actually receive gambling proceeds earmarked for them.
- Fair advertising about odds and payouts.

Is gambling good for us or bad? There is no clear-cut answer because it's both; sometimes more one than the other. It's up to individuals to take a stand on each issue associated with gambling and decide for themselves what is beneficial and what is harmful. People can take action by contacting their legislative representatives and making their beliefs and feelings about the issues known. People can also vote the way they believe and campaign for what they believe is right.

For more information about gambling or help for compulsive gamblers, contact:

- Gamblers Anonymous, P.O. Box 17173, Los Angeles, CA 90017, 213-386-8789.
- National Council on Problem Gambling, 445 West 59th Street, New York, NY 10019, 800-522-4700.

# Glossary

**action**—To have a bet; total of all wagers made.

**bank**—The person who controls the money in a card game.

**bankroll**—The amount of money a person has to gamble.

**bookmaker**—A person who takes illegal bets; also called a bookie.

**cage**—The main casino cashier.

**compulsive gambler**—A person who cannot control his or her betting activities.

**folding money**—Currency.

**high roller**—Anyone who gambles $5,000 or more.

**hit**—To ask for another card in 21.

**house advantage**—The mathematical odds the house uses to ensure it makes a profit.

**juice**—Knowing influential people; having influence or power.

**limit**—The amount you can bet.

**lock**—A bet that is a "sure-thing."

**long shot**—A bet that has low odds of winning.

**office**—Where bets are placed.

**pit**—The employee-only areas behind gaming tables.

**pot**—The money bet on each hand of poker.

**push**—A bet that doesn't win or lose.

**runner**—A person who works for a bookie and who collects bets and makes payoffs.

**sharp**—A cheating gambler.

**shill**—A person who lures others into making wagers.

**stiff**—A winner who doesn't tip the dealer.

**take**—Gambling income.

# Chapter Notes

## Chapter 1

1. Art Levine, "Playing the Adolescent Odds," *U.S. News & World Report,* June 18, 1990, p. 51.

2. Ricardo Chivara, "The Rise of Teenage Gambling," *Time,* February 25, 1991, p. 78.

3. Ibid.

4. Michael Marr, "PogMania: A Tale of an Industry Gone Wild," *Collector MilkCaps Illustrated,* February 1995, p. 11.

5. Unless otherwise noted, information for the section on compulsive gambling comes from the following sources:

*Adolescent Compulsive Gambling,* The Council on Compulsive Gambling of New Jersey, Inc. (brochure).

*Compulsive Gambling,* The Council on Compulsive Gambling of New Jersey, Inc. (brochure).

*Is Gambling Running the Rest of Your Life?* The Council on Compulsive Gambling of New Jersey.

Peter Finch, "Confessions of a Compulsive High Roller," *Business Week,* July 29, 1991, p. 78.

Dan Cordtz, "Betting the Country," *FW,* February 20, 1990, p. 23.

Linda Berman, M.S.W., and Mary-Ellen Siegel, M.S.W., *Behind the Eight-Ball* (New York: Fireside Parkside Recovery Books, 1992), pp. 30–31, 69–78, 80–85, 100–101, 239, 245.

Michelle Ingrassia, "Betting: When It Becomes a Problem," *Newsweek,* June 14, 1993, p. 74.

Gwenda Blair, "Betting Against the Odds," *The New York Time Magazine,* September 25, 1988, pp. 57, 76.

Deke Castleman, *Las Vegas* (California: Compass American Guides, 1993), pp. 138–139.

Sue Berkman, "When Gambling Becomes a Disease," *Good Housekeeping,* January 1991, p. 169.

Ann Magnuson, "Going for Broke," *Bazaar,* February 1995, p. 188.

Iris Cohen Selinger, "The Big Lottery Gamble," *Advertising Age,* May 10, 1993, p. 26.

*Compulsive Gambling,* The Council on Compulsive Gambling of New Jersey.

6. Castleman, pp. 138–139.

7. Finch, pp. 78–79.

8. Berkman, p. 169.

9. Ingrassia, p. 74.

10. Blair, p. 57.

11. Levine, p. 51.

12. Levine, p. 51.

13. Interview with Ed Looney, executive director, The Council on Compulsive Gambling of New Jersey, Inc.

14. Peter Hellman, "Casino Craze," *Travel Holiday,* March 1994, pp. 80–81; James Popkin and Katia Hetter, "America's Gambling Craze," *U.S. News & World Report,* March 14, 1994, pp. 42–46; and Levine, p. 51.

15. Jerry Adler, Karen Springen, Daniel Glick, "Just Say Yes, Hit Me Again," *Newsweek,* June 21, 1993, p. 69.

## Chapter 2

1. Pauline Yoshishashi, "The Gambling Industry Rakes It In As Casinos Spread Across the U.S.," *The Wall Street Journal,* October 22, 1993, p. A-9.

2. David Spanier, *Easy Money: Inside the Gambler's Mind* (London: Secker and Warburg, 1987), p. 131.

3. Unless otherwise noted, all historical references and anecdotes come from the following sources:

J. M. Fenster, "Nation of Gamblers," *American Heritage,* September 1994, pp. 34–50.

John M. Findlay, *People of Chance* (New York: Oxford University Press, 1986).

Carol D. Foster, Nancy R. Jacobs, Mark A. Siegel, editors, *Gambling—Crime or Recreation* (Plano, Tex.: Instructional Aides, Inc., 1984).

John Steele Gordon, "Born in Iniquity," *American Heritage,* February/March 1994, pp. 14–16.

Jim Haskins, *Gambling—Who Really Wins?* (New York: Franklin Watts, 1979).

Hank Messick and Burt Goldblatt, *The Only Game in Town* (New York: Thomas Y. Crowell Company, 1976).

Richard Sasuly, *Bookies and Bettors* (New York: Holt, Rinehart and Winston, 1982).

4. Peter Hellman, "Casino Craze," *Travel Holiday,* March 1994, p. 146.

5. Interview with Ed Looney, executive director, The Council on Compulsive Gambling of New Jersey, Inc.

6. Yoshishashi, p. A-9.

7. Ibid., p. A-1.

8. Gordon Williams, "Investor or Gambler?," *FW,* January 18, 1994, p. 70; and Ed Looney, *Stock Market Gambling,* paper.

9. Williams, p. 70.

10. Linda Berman, M.S.W., and Mary-Ellen Siegel, M.S.W., *Behind the Eight-Ball,* (New York: Fireside Parkside Recovery Books, 1992), pp. 30–31.

## Chapter 3

1. Unless otherwise noted, information on lotteries comes from the following sources:

George Will, "In the Grip of Gambling," *Newsweek,* May 8, 1989, p. 78.

Jennifer Vogel, "A Lotto Bunk," *Utne Reader,* November/December 1993, p. 19.

Paul Magnusson, "A National Lottery Is Not Such a Long Shot," *Business Week,* April 10, 1989, p. 57.

Bonnie Angelo, "Life at the End of the Rainbow," *Time,* November 4, 1991, p. 80.

Erik Calonius, "The Big Payoff from Lotteries," *Fortune,* March 25, 1991, p. 109.

Dan Cordtz, "Betting the Country," *FW,* February 20, 1990, p. 25.

Iris Cohen Selinger, "The Big Lottery Gamble," *Advertising Age,* May 10, 1993, p. 26.

James Cook, "Legalizing the Slots," *Forbes,* March 2, 1992, pp. 78–79.

2. Calonius, p. 113.

3. Vogel, p. 19.

4. Angelo, p. 80.

5. Will, p. 78.

6. Cook, pp. 78–79.

7. Magnusson, p. 57.

8. Ibid.

9. Selinger, p. 25.

10. Cordtz, p. 28

11. Selinger, p. 26.

12. Unless otherwise noted, information on casinos comes from the following sources:

Deke Castleman, *Las Vegas* (California: Compass American Guides, 1993), p. 12.

Barney Vinson, *Las Vegas Behind the Tables* (Michigan: Gollehon Press, 1988), pp. 55–81, 89; Castleman, pp. 161, 165.

Darwin Orkin, *Gambling Scams: How They Work, How to Detect Them, How to Protect Yourself* (New York: Carol Publishing, 1990), pp. 55–75.

Ann Magnuson, "Going for Broke," *Bazaar,* February 1995, p. 184.

13. Castleman, pp. 59–60.

14. Unless otherwise noted, information on casino games comes from Castleman and Vinson.

15. Magnuson, p. 184.

16. Vinson, p. 62.

17. Vinson, pp. 73, 201, 212; and the Las Vegas Visitors and Convention Bureau.

18. Ibid., p. 217.

## Chapter 4

1. George Sternlieb and James W. Hughes, *The Atlantic City Gamble* (Cambridge, MA: Harvard University Press, 1983), p. 7.

2. Ibid., p. ix.

3. David Spanier, *Easy Money: Inside the Gambler's Mind* (London: Secker and Warburg, 1987), p. 187.

4. Ibid., p. 4.

5. Unless otherwise noted, information about Native American casinos comes from the following sources:

Spanier, pp. 188–89.

Peter Hellman, "Casino Craze," *Travel Holiday,* March 1994, p. 88.

"Buffalo Stakes," *The Economist,* July 24, 1993, pp. 25–26.

Dirk Johnson, "Economies Come to Life on Indian Reservations," *The New York Times,* July 3, 1991, p. A-1.

Harvey Shapiro, "A Full House: Gambling," *Hemispheres,* October 1994, p. 80.

6. Ibid. p. 83.

7. Johnson, p. A-1.

8. Ibid.

9. The report of the Mohawk war comes from Daniel D'Ambrosio, "Incident at Akwesasne," *Gentleman's Quarterly,* November 1993, pp. 217–270.

10. Ibid.

11. Unless otherwise noted, information in this section comes from the following sources:

Pauline Yoshishashi, "The Gambling Industry Rakes It In As Casinos Spread Across the U.S.," *The Wall Street Journal,* October 22, 1993, p. A-9.

Gerri Hirshey, "Gambling Nation," *The New York Times Magazine,* July 17, 1994, p. 40.

"Buffalo Stakes," p. 25.

James Popkin with Katia Hetter, "America's Gambling Craze," *U.S. News & World Report*, March 14, 1994, p. 42.

12. Yoshishashi, p. A-9.

13. Hirshey, p. 40.

14. Hellman, p. 84.

15. Ibid., p. 41.

16. Yoshishashi, p. A-9.

## Chapter 5

1. Unless otherwise noted, the information on gambling parents and siblings comes from the following source:

Linda Berman, M.S.W., and Mary-Ellen Siegel, M.S.W., *Behind the Eight-Ball* (New York: Fireside Parkside Recovery Books, 1992), pp. 80–83, 100–101, 239, 245.

2. Jerry Adler, Karen Springen, Daniel Glick, "Just Say Yes, Hit Me Again," *Newsweek,* June 21, 1993, pp. 68–69.

3. *Adolescent Compulsive Gambling,* The Council on Compulsive Gambling of New Jersey.

4. *Compulsive Gambling,* The Council on Compulsive Gambling of New Jersey.

5. "'Til Death Do Us Part," *The Economist,* February 19, 1994, p. 30; and "Cockfighting," *The Humane Society of the United States Fact Sheets,* September 1991.

6. "'Til Death Do Us Part," p. 30.

7. Kathy Strain, "Greyhound Racing," *Mainstream,* Spring 1992, pp. 20–23; and "Dog Racing," *Humane Society of the United States Fact Sheet.*

8. David Johnston, "The Dark Side of Charity Gambling," *Money,* October 1993, pp. 130–136.

9. Unless otherwise noted, information on crime and gambling comes from the following sources:

"Pari-Mutuel Gambling and Organized Crime," Greyhound Friends for Life.

Interview with Ed Looney, executive director, Council on Compulsive Gambling of New Jersey.

Darwin Ortiz, *Gambling Scams: How They Work, How To Detect Them, How To Protect Yourself* (New York: Carol Publishing, 1990), p. 34.

John McCormack, "Chicago's Modern Mob," *Newsweek,* May 11, 1987, p. 35.

Selwin Raab, "Faxes Produce Numbers Arrest in Harlem Ring," *The New York Times,* April 21, 1994, p. B-1, B-4.

10. "Pari-Mutuel Gambling and Organized Crime."

11. Ortiz, p. 57.

12. Ibid., p. 156.

13. Ibid., p. 193.

# Bibliography

## Sources

Ed Looney, executive director, Council on Compulsive Gambling of New Jersey, 609-599-3299, interview; and Looney, ed. "Stock Market Gambling" (paper).

Susan Netboy, regional coordinator, Greyhound Friends for Life, 415-851-7812. Reports: "Pari-Mutuel Gambling and Organized Crime," "Pari-Mutuel Gambling and Socioeconomic Factors."

## Books

Berman, Linda, M.S.W., and Mary-Ellen Siegel, M.S.W. *Behind the Eight-Ball.* New York: Fireside Parkside Recovery Books, 1992.

Castleman, Deke. *Las Vegas.* California: Compass American Guides, 1993.

Findlay, John M. *People of Chance.* New York: Oxford University Press, 1986. Foster, Carol D., Nancy R. Jacobs, and Mark A. Siegel, editors. *Gambling—Crime or Recreation.* Plano, TX: Instructional Aides, Inc., 1984.

Haskins, Jim. *Gambling—Who Really Wins?* New York: Franklin Watts, 1979.

Messick, Hank, and Burt Goldblatt. *The Only Game in Town.* New York: Thomas Y. Crowell Company, 1976.

Orkin, Michael. *Can You Win? The Real Odds for Casino Gambling, Sports Betting, and Lotteries.* U.S.A.: W. H. Freeman and Company, 1991.

Ortiz, Darwin. *Gambling Scams; How They Work, How To Detect Them, How To Protect Yourself.* New York: Carol Publishing, 1990.

Sasuly, Richard. *Bookies and Bettors.* New York: Holt, Rinehart, Winston, 1982.

Spanier, David. *Easy Money: Inside the Gambler's Mind.* London: Secker and Warburg, 1987.

Sternlieb, George, and James W. Hughes. *The Atlantic City Gamble.* Cambridge, MA: Harvard University Press, 1983.

Vinson, Barney. *Las Vegas Behind the Tables* and *Las Vegas Behind the Tables Part 2.* Michigan: Gollehon Press, 1988 and 1989, respectively.

## Brochures

*Adolescent Compulsive Gambling.* The Council on Compulsive Gambling of New Jersey.

*Compulsive Gambling.* The Council on Compulsive Gambling of New Jersey.

*Humane Society of the United States Fact Sheets.* "Cockfighting," "Dog Racing."

*Humane Society of the United States Special Report.* "Cockfighting."

*Is Gambling Running the Rest of Your Life?* The Council on Compulsive Gambling of New Jersey.

## Periodicals

"A Punt on the River," *The Economist* (March 13, 1993), 37. "'Til Death Us Do Part." *The Economist* (February 19, 1994), 30.

"A Town That Turned the Desert Green." *U.S. News & World Report* (July 2, 1990), 11.

"As Vote Nears Detroit Edges Closer to Gambling." *The New York Times* (July 24, 1994).

"Buffalo Stakes." *The Economist* (July 24, 1993), 25–26.

"Bugsy and the Indians." *The Economist* (March 21, 1992), 27–28.

"Don't Let the U.S. Become One Big Casino." *Business Week* (April 24, 1989), 160.

"Football Pools Proliferate Despite Banning Office Betting." *The Wall Street Journal* (September 13, 1994), A-1.

"Running Wide Open." *ASPCA Report* (Winter 1992), 17–19.

Adler, Jerry, Karen Springen, Daniel Glick, "Just Say Yes, Hit Me Again." *Newsweek* (June 21, 1993), 68–69.

Anderson, Kurt. "Las Vegas, U.S.A." *Time* (January 10, 1994), 42–51.

Angelo, Bonnie. "Life at the End of the Rainbow." *Time* (November 4, 1991), 80–81.

Baker, James, with Debra Rosenberg and Susan Miller. "Gambling on the Reservation." *Newsweek* (February 17, 1992), 29.

Baker, James, with Karen Springen. "Gambling on Riverboats." *Newsweek* (February 5, 1990), 76.

Berkman, Sue. "When Gambling Becomes a Disease." *Good Housekeeping* (January 1991), 169.

Blair, Gwenda. "Betting Against the Odds." *The New York Times Magazine* (September 25, 1988), 57–91.

Briancon, Pierre. "Mirror on the U.S." *World Press Review* (December 1993), 36–37.

Calonius, Erik. "The Big Payoff from Lotteries." *Fortune* (March 25, 1991), 109–114.

Came, Barry. "The Big Payoff." *McClean's* (January 17, 1994), 17–18. Chivara, Ricardo. "The Rise of Teenage Gambling." *Time* (February 25, 1991), 78.

Coleman, Calmetta. "Is Casino Gambling in West Baden, Ind., Answer to a Prayer?" *The Wall Street Journal* (August 26, 1994), A-1.

Cook, James. "Legalizing the Slots." *Forbes* (March 2, 1992), 78–79.

Cordtz, Dan. "Betting the Country." *FW* (February 20, 1990), 23–26.

Corelli, Rae. "Betting on Casinos." *McClean's* (May 30, 1994), 26–29.

D'Ambrosio, Daniel. "Incident at Akwesasne." *Gentleman's Quarterly* (November 1993), 217–270.

Fenster, J. M. "Nation of Gamblers." *American Heritage* (September 1994), 34–50.

Finch, Peter. "Confessions of a Compulsive High Roller." *Business Week* (July 29, 1991), 78.

Fost, Dan. "Fear and Marketing in Las Vegas." *American Demographics* (October 1993), 19–20.

Gordon, John Steele. "Born in Iniquity." *American Heritage* (February/March 1994), 14–16.

Gubernick, Lisa. "The Pied Pipers of Vegas." *Forbes* (December 6, 1993), 235–236.

Hellman, Peter. "Casino Craze." *Travel Holiday* (March 1994), 80–147.

Hirshey, Gerri. "Gambling Nation." *The New York Times Magazine* (July 17, 1994), 34–61.

Hull, Tupper. "Odds Favor Gambling Laws." *San Francisco Examiner* (December 4, 1994), C-4.

Ingrassia, Michelle. "Betting: When It Becomes a Problem." *Newsweek* (June 14, 1993), 74.

Johnson, Dirk. "Economies Come to Life on Indian Reservations." *The New York Times* (July 3, 1991), A-1, 18.

Johnston, David. "The Dark Side of Charity Gambling." *Money* (October 1993), 130–136.

Karp, Jonathan. "Video Bandits." *Far Eastern Economic Review* (January 1992), 33.

Kirshenbaum, Jerry, editor. "Scorecard." *Sports Illustrated* (June 14, 1993), 13.

Konik, Michael. "Shakin' Down the Sheiks." *Forbes* (January 3, 1994), 152–155.

Levine, Art. "Playing the Adolescent Odds." *U.S. News & World Report* (June 18, 1990), 51.

McCormack, John. "Chicago's Modern Mob: A Home in the Suburbs." *Newsweek* (May 11, 1987), 35.

Magnuson, Ann. "Going for Broke." *Bazaar* (February 1995), 184–224.

Magnusson, Paul. "A National Lottery Is Not Such a Long Shot." *Business Week* (April 10, 1989), 57.

Marr, Michael. "PogMania: A Tale of an Industry Gone Wild." *Collector MilkCaps Illustrated* (February 1995), 9–23.

Marshall, Jonathan. "Gambling Fever." *San Francisco Chronicle* (May 9, 1994), D-3.

Murray, William. "Magic City." *Travel Holiday* (October 1994).

Painton, Priscilla. "The Great Casino Salesman." *Time* (May 3, 1993), 52–55.

Popkin, James. "Tricks of the Trade." and "A Mixed Blessing for 'America's Ethiopia'." *U.S. News & World Report* (March 14, 1994), 48–56.

Popkin, James with Katia Hetter. "America's Gambling Craze." *U.S. News & World Report* (March 14, 1994), 42–46.

Raab, Selwin. "Faxes Produce Numbers Arrest in Harlem Ring." *The New York Times* (April 21, 1994), B-1, B-4.

Reilly, Rick. "Smells Like Another Rose." *Sports Illustrated* (June 21, 1993), 74.

Ritter, John. "Detroit Rolls the Dice on Casino Gambling." *USA Today* (August 2, 1994), 2A.

Rosen, Margery. "My Husband Is a Compulsive Gambler." *Ladies Home Journal* (April 1994), 15–18.

Seligman, Daniel. "Legalizing Raymond." *Fortune* (May 30, 1994), 173.

Selinger, Iris Cohen. "The Big Lottery Gamble." *Advertising Age* (May 10, 1993), 25–29.

Serwer, Andrew. "Welcome to the New Las Vegas." *Fortune* (January 24, 1994), 102–105.

Shapiro, Harvey. "A Full House: Gambling." *Hemispheres* (October 1994), 78–86.

Strain, Kathy. "Greyhound Racing." *Mainstream* (Spring 1992), 20–23.

Vogel, Jennifer. "A Lotto Bunk." *Utne Reader* (November/December 1993), 18–23.

Will, George. "In the Grip of Gambling." *Newsweek* (May 8, 1989), 78.

Williams, Gordon. "Investor or Gambler?" *FW* (January 18, 1994), 70–71.

Yoshishashi, Pauline. "The Gambling Industry Rakes It in as Casinos Spread Across the U.S." *The Wall Street Journal* (October 22, 1993), A-1, A-9.

# Index